Napoleon's
Eighty Days

Napoleon's Eighty Days

D. J. GOODSPEED

HOUGHTON MIFFLIN COMPANY BOSTON

The Riverside Press Cambridge

1965

ACKNOWLEDGMENT

The author is glad to acknowledge his indebtedness to Mr. John Eldred Howard for permission to quote from the translations contained in Volume I of his *Letters and Documents of Napoleon*, published by the Cresset Press, London.

C

First Printing

Printed in the United States of America

Contents

Illustrations

Letizia Bonaparte

Napoleon

Josephine

Napoleon as 1st Consul

Mme Récamier

Joseph Bonaparte

Charles Bernadotte

Prologue

On 14th July 1789, a Paris mob, led by a handful of mutinous soldiers, stormed and took the Bastille. That ancient building, half fortress, half prison, and the visible symbol of the power of the 1300-year-old French monarchy, was only indifferently defended, and when the mob broke in they found it almost empty. Nevertheless, the fall of the Bastille shook every throne in Europe. The French Revolution had begun, and for the next quarter of a century the entire continent was to ring with the clash of arms. Before peace returned, millions were to die, nations were to be convulsed in agony, and the history of the world was to be wrenched violently and forever from its accustomed course.

Less than two months after the taking of the Bastille, a National Assembly, the first ever to meet in France, declared that all Frenchmen had a natural right to liberty, equality, property and security; feudalism was abolished; seigniorial privileges done away with; and the royal power drastically limited. The king and queen were held as virtual prisoners in the Tuileries, and the following June when they attempted to escape, they were recaptured at Varennes and ignominiously brought back to the capital.

Foreign wars followed hard on internal revolt. An invading Prussian army was turned back at Valmy in September 1792, but not before the threat of military defeat had increased the tempo of revolution in France. Twelve hundred helpless prisoners

9

were butchered in the dungeons of Paris that September; the monarchy was abolished; and on 21st January 1793, the bumbling, good-hearted Louis XVI had his head cut off in the Place de la Révolution.

Each month thereafter the weighted wheel of revolution spun faster, as it received new impetus from the mounting fears and passions of men caught up in events too momentous for them to control. The National Convention divided into two parties, the Girondists and the extreme Left-wing Jacobins under Maximilien Robespierre. Inevitably, as violence begat violence and murder led to murder, the extremists inherited the power of the state. A terrible fear settled on Paris, and spread from Paris to the provinces. The members of the Committee of Public Safety, by now the real rulers of France, were also afraid—afraid of invasion, afraid of royalist conspiracies, afraid of slipping down the bloody slope they had so desperately climbed, and, most of all, afraid of the people they claimed to represent. In its fear the Committee struck out wildly on all sides. By June 1794 the triangular knife of the guillotine was killing nearly seven hundred people each month; in July there was an appalling total of nine hundred and thirty-five executions. Paris reeked of blood.

It could not possibly continue, and on 28th July Robespierre himself was outlawed, dragged wounded from his refuge in the Hôtel de Ville, and guillotined, together with many of the leading Jacobins. After Robespierre's death France paused, exhausted. There had been five years of murderous chaos and now the nation attempted to call a halt to its furious revolutionary violence. A new constitution was promulgated in October 1795, providing for an executive of five Directors and for two legislative bodies, the Council of Five Hundred and the Council of Ancients.

Yet the flow of blood was not to be staunched so easily. While the Government of France had weakened itself with intrigue and murder, the army had become an increasingly important political factor. Symptomatic of the army's influence was the fact that the new constitution could be put into effect only after a young

Corsican general, Napoleon Bonaparte, had turned his guns on the Paris mob. It is dangerous for Governments to have to rely thus upon soldiers, and the Directory did what it could to lessen the danger. In March 1796 General Bonaparte was promoted to take command of the Army of Italy, ostensibly as a reward, but more probably to get him out of France.

South of the Alps, 1796 was a year of military miracles. The Corsican general, waging a kind of war the world had never seen before, won victory after victory. He moved with a speed and sureness unrivalled since the campaigns of Caesar. Austrian armies were beaten time and time again, and when peace came the name of Napoleon Bonaparte was as frightening to the five Directors as it was to the Austrian generals.

Although Britain had joined the Coalition against France, by 1798 the Revolution seemed more secure from its external foes than at any time in the past nine years. Even so, the suggestion now put forward by Talleyrand that France send an expedition to Egypt was strategically unsound. The plan for the expedition is said to have come from the archives of the old royalist Ministry of War, but to send a picked French army to Africa while the hostile British fleet still controlled the Mediterranean was foolhardy. For different reasons, however, both General Bonaparte and the Directory were immediately attracted to the idea. The Directors were anxious to be rid of a potentially dangerous general, and Bonaparte, in turn, felt that if he stayed too long inactive in France, his garlands would soon wither. There was, too, as Talleyrand had probably guessed, a nobler reason for Bonaparte's strategic error. For as long as he could remember he had had an almost mystical feeling about the East. The lands that had been conquered by Alexander the Great were bound up in his mind with his own boyhood, the happy time when dreams had never been compromised by coming true.

Thus, on 19th May 1798, a French army of forty thousand men sailed in four hundred transports from Toulon and other nearby Mediterranean ports. General Bonaparte went with the army as its Commander-in-Chief, and all five of the Directors were relieved when they heard that he was gone.

PART ONE

The Return of the Hero

THE HOT August night pressed closely in around the cove. There was no moon, and the stars did little to relieve the blackness. Down by the beach, where the waves broke white against the dark sand, the air was sharp with the salty smell of the sea. Three miles to the east, still on the seashore but hidden from sight by a low, sandy ridge, the lights of Alexandria reflected in faint luminescence from the sky, like a patch of false dawn.

In the cove, a few cable-lengths from shore, two small warships rode at anchor, snubbing at their chains. The *Muiron* and *Carrère* were both old vessels, Venetian-built frigates carrying twenty-two guns a side, slow-sailers that had been pressed into French service some years before. They were slightly larger than the French forty-fours, but handled less easily because of their shallower draught. Farther out in Marabout Bay were two tiny corvettes, the *Revanche* and the *Fortune,* trim, copper-bottomed vessels, faster than the frigates but lightly armed.[1] Tonight the sails of all four ships were furled tight on their yards; gun-ports were closed; and no riding-lights glowed on the mastheads.

Except for a few shaded lanterns, the ships lay in darkness; but on the waters of the cove an assortment of small craft plied to and fro between the jetty and the frigates. Jolly-boats, cutters, gigs, and launches, all packed to the gunwales with soldiers, made their way out to the warships to discharge their passengers and

return empty for another load. The soldiers wore turbans and
burnouses, but their green jackets marked them as the *chasseurs
à cheval* of the Guides, the personal bodyguard of the French
Commander-in-Chief.

On shore, not far from the waiting ranks of Guides, a short
thin man in a plain green tunic watched this secret embarkation.
His hands were clasped behind his back and his chin thrust
forward on his chest as though to rest a head too heavy with
thought. Around him clustered a group of general officers and
their aides-de-camp.

It was the night of 22nd August 1799, and General Napoleon
Bonaparte, Commander-in-Chief of the Army of Egypt, was
about to leave that army behind him and attempt the perilous
voyage back to France through seas blockaded by the British
fleet.

As the *Muiron* and *Carrère* were hastily loaded with the picked
men of the Guides, the French could see the outline of an English
brig lying offshore as though observing the preparations for
departure.[2] The odds were long against Bonaparte's being able to
slip safely through the British cordon. Admiral Nelson's main
fleet, based on Syracuse, kept close watch over the narrow stretch
of sea between Marsala in Sicily and Cape Bon. Moreover, for
all the General knew, the sinister little brig which had appeared
off Marabout Bay at three o'clock that afternoon might be the
watchdog for a squadron of Sir Sidney Smith's cruisers just over
the horizon. If the brig was still there in the morning, Bonaparte
would have to postpone his sailing.

If that happened, the consequences might well be incalculable.
The Army of Egypt was in serious difficulties. The African
expedition had never been popular either with officers or men,
and a mutinous mood had been apparent ever since the French
had landed on 1st July 1798. Many of the more thoughtful
officers believed that, because of the supremacy of the British
fleet, the entire strategic concept of striking a blow at England
through the East had always been chimerical. On the march to

Cairo, across the hot sands, the soldiers had died by hundreds of thirst, hunger and heat. Some of them, seeing the sufferings of their comrades, had blown out their brains; others had thrown themselves into the Nile to drown. An easy victory over the Mamelukes at the Battle of the Pyramids had not reconciled the French to the Egyptian campaign. Certainly, ever since that summer evening a year ago when Nelson had crashed through the French line of battle in Aboukir Bay, raking de Bruey's anchored vessels until they burned or struck their colours, the position of the French Army had been patently hopeless. Africa had been turned into a gigantic trap.

The Commander-in-Chief had considered three possible ways out of the trap—marching south-east to India, marching west to Ceuta opposite Gibraltar, or marching back to France by way of Syria and Constantinople. None of the three courses had really been feasible but Bonaparte had chosen the least hazardous. The army had set out for Syria in the dead of winter across three hundred miles of bleak desert. In May, having failed to take the fortress of St Jean d'Acre, the French were forced to retreat back to Egypt, weaker by five thousand men. The trap was now obvious to everyone, and the army was not deceived by the General's misleading bulletins which attempted to explain away the Syrian fiasco.

In July 1799 the Turks had landed an expeditionary force at Aboukir Bay, and Bonaparte had advanced to attack. The night before the battle, the French artist Rigaut had lain awake, observing the commander-in-chief:

> [Rigaut] said he was never near Bonaparte but he was attracted by his physiognomy; there was something in his face so acute, so thoughtful, so terrible, that it always impressed him, and that this night, when all the rest were buried in sleep, he could not avoid watching him. In a little time he observed Napoleon take the compasses and a chart of Aboukir and the Mediterranean and measure, and then take a ruler and draw lines. He then arose, went to the door of his tent and looked toward the horizon; then returned to

his tent and looked at his watch; after a moment he took a knife, and cut the table in all ways like a boy. He then rested his head on his hand, looked again at his watch for some time, went again to the door of his tent, and again returned to his seat. There was something peculiarly awful in the circumstances—the time of night—his generals soundly sleeping—Bonaparte's strong features lighted up by a lamp—the feeling that the Turks were encamped near them, and that before long a dreadful battle would be fought . . . In a short time Napoleon called them all up, ordered his horse, and asked how long before daybreak.[3]

The next day, Bonaparte with six thousand men annihilated the Turkish army of eighteen thousand, but in spite of this spectacular victory, generals and private soldiers alike murmured that the real purpose of their presence in Egypt was to augment Bonaparte's personal glory and that for once the Commander-in-Chief's soaring imagination was out of proportion with reality. They mistrusted his dreams of emulating Alexander the Great and were suspicious of the high poetry of some of his public utterances. Before the battle of Aboukir, for instance, he had said that the coming engagement " would decide the history of the world ", and after the battle of the Pyramids he had told his soldiers that they had won a victory " with forty centuries looking down ".[4]

This sort of thing was all very well; but now, after fourteen months in the East, the Army had been reduced by one half; the troops were four million francs behind in their pay; the plague was raging in their ranks; and they hated the dirt, flies, heat and dysentery of Egypt. Most of them despaired of seeing France again. If they were to discover that only the presence of an English brig off Marabout Bay had prevented Bonaparte from deserting them, there might be serious trouble.

Bonaparte had made his decision almost a month before. After the battle of Aboukir, he had sent one of his officers aboard Sir Sidney Smith's flagship on the pretext of treating for the ransom of prisoners. The brilliant, erratic admiral had received the French

envoy with elaborate courtesy, and among other gifts had presented him with a bundle of old newspapers. Probably on this
occasion Sir Sidney Smith's graciousness was not entirely disinterested. For the past ten months no news from Europe had
reached the French Army, and the discontent prevalent in its
ranks would surely be increased by the reports in these journals of
serious French defeats in Italy and on the Rhine.

If this was the calculation, it succeeded, and in succeeding
failed disastrously. The French Army was certainly demoralized as
a result of Sir Sidney Smith's gift, but the commander of that
army, who was never demoralized, countered with the action by
which he was to dominate the history of Europe for the next
sixteen years.

General Bonaparte had stayed up all that night in his tent,
reading and thinking. From a copy of the *French Gazette* published in Frankfurt on 6th June 1799, he learned that the im-
placable enemies of France were again closing in upon her frontiers. The kings of Europe would make no lasting peace with
the Republic, and England, Austria, Russia and Turkey had
formed a new coalition. Most of the territory Bonaparte had
taken from Austria in his Italian campaign of 1796 had been lost;
Generals Jourdan and Bernadotte had been defeated by the
Austrian Archduke Charles at Stockach and had promptly retired
west of the Rhine; the Russian commander Suvarov was threatening the French bastion in Switzerland; and in several departments
of France itself there was civil war. On the other hand, Bonaparte's despatch telling of the annihilation of the Turks at Aboukir
would reach France at an ideal moment. His account of victories
in Egypt, exaggerated and falsified though it was,[5] would appear
in happy contrast to the defeats of the other Republican generals.
And if, as seemed likely, a political upheaval were to result from
the series of French disasters in Europe, it would be a pity not to
be in Paris at the time. *Les absents ont toujours tort.*

All night the General slumped in his chair in the tent, his
legs spread out and his head on his breast, while behind his

eyes picture after picture formed and possibility after possibility.

With the morning Bonaparte called for his old schoolfriend and secretary, Bourrienne, and exclaimed: " The fools have lost Italy! All the fruits of our victories are gone! I must leave Egypt! "[6] He ordered the *Muiron* and *Carrère* to be provisioned in the greatest secrecy with four months' supplies and three months' water for four hundred men.*

Originally only Bourrienne, Berthier, the chief-of-staff, and Admiral Ganteaume had been let into the secret. Some time later the General confided in another old friend, Marmont, the commandant of Alexandria.[7] Quietly and furtively the ships were victualled and assembled in Marabout Bay. It was as vital to conceal the plan from the French Army as from the English Navy, but in spite of all precautions, vague rumours leaked out. General Dugua, the commandant of Cairo, wrote asking permission to issue an official denial. Bonaparte did not reply to this letter, but announced that he was shortly setting out for a tour of the Delta.[8]

On 13th August, Admiral Ganteaume had reported that the ships would be ready for sea by the twentieth, but had added that he doubted whether the voyage could be made with any prospect of success before November, when the long nights and favourable south winds would be helpful. Six days later, at five o'clock in the morning, a despatch-rider, who had travelled hard and fast from Alexandria by camel, awakened General Bonaparte with an urgent message. Admiral Ganteaume sent news of unexpected good fortune: Sir Sidney Smith's fleet had disappeared.[9]†

Bonaparte had made up his mind on the instant. That same

---

* The French historian, P. Lanfrey, claims that Bonaparte had learned of the disasters in Italy some twelve days earlier, when he received a letter dated 26th May 1799, from three of the Directors, Barras, Rewbell and Larevellière-Lépeaux. According to Lanfrey, a Greek courier brought this letter secretly to Bonaparte via Tunis and Tripoli. The weight of evidence, however, appears to favour Bourrienne's version. In any case, the point is immaterial except insofar as Lanfrey's story supports his general thesis of Napoleon's habitual duplicity.

† Smith had, in fact, sailed to Cyprus to take on water.

day Berthier had written to Desaix, Kléber, Menou, Murat, Marmont and Bessières, ordering them to meet the Commander-in-Chief as soon as possible at Rosetta, near Alexandria.

It had been impossible for General Kléber to reach Rosetta in time to keep his rendezvous with the Commander-in-Chief, and perhaps Bonaparte was as well pleased that this was so. At all events, on the day of the embarkation Bonaparte wrote to Kléber, explaining that he was forced to sail two or three days sooner than he had intended. He appointed Kléber to command the Army and, along with much sound advice, gave that unfortunate soldier permission, should the plague kill one thousand five hundred of his men, " to conclude peace with the Ottoman Porte, even if the evacuation of Egypt has to be the principal condition." Among the many instructions Bonaparte gave Kléber, was this significant sentence: " You will find attached a cipher for correspondence with the Government and another for correspondence with me."[10]

General Bonaparte told his soldiers of his departure in a short bulletin which closed with this paragraph:

> The Army will soon have news of me; I can say no more. It is hard for me to leave the soldiers to whom I am most attached; but it will be only for a time, and the new Commander-in-Chief has the confidence of the Government and of myself.[11]

It would be tomorrow before the Army read this announcement, and by then the ships would have sailed. Now, on the beach, the General turned to his young stepson and aide-de-camp, Eugene Beauharnais, playfully pinched his ear, and said:

" Well, Eugene, you're going to see your mother again."[12]

In truth, perhaps only Bonaparte felt no regret at leaving Egypt. The others were glad enough to be going home, but they did not much like the stealthy method of their departure and they felt some remorse at leaving their comrades behind.[13] But the young General was too concerned with the future to sentimentalize over the past. Later, as Emperor, he was to abandon another

Army after having led it into an impossible position. In thirteen years' time, however, he was to lose some of the knack of the plausible farewell. When he left the *Grande Armée* to die in the snows of Russia while he whisked back to France in the sled with Caulaincourt, his valedictory bulletin was to close fantastically with the words: "His Majesty's health has never been better."[14]

Between the flight from Egypt and the flight from Russia there was to be nothing but an epic. The man remained the same. And on the night of 22nd August 1799, General Bonaparte may well have reflected that most of the Army of Egypt was rabidly republican. Many of the officers were almost Jacobins. It might be as well if this Army stayed out of France for a spell.

In any case, the Egyptian expedition had failed. Whatever he might say to the Army, Bonaparte was far too intellectually honest not to admit this fact to himself. In later years, on St Helena, he was to refer to Sir Sidney Smith, who had successfully blocked his advance at St Jean d'Acre, as the man who "made me miss my destiny."[15] Now it was time to cut his losses.

Late on the night of 22nd August, Bonaparte and his senior officers were ferried out to the frigates. With Admiral Ganteaume on the *Muiron* went the General himself, his stepson Eugene, Berthier, Bourrienne, General Andréossy, and the savants of the Institute, Monge and Berthollet. With Captain Dumanoir on the *Carrère* went Murat, Lannes, Bessières, Marmont, and the artist Denon.[16]

In the future, five of these men were to become marshals of the Empire. The sallow-faced little General whose star they had already learned to follow was soon to be an Emperor, ruling a territory greater than ever Charlemagne controlled. They themselves were to share his fortune. One of them, Murat, was to become a king; Berthier was to become twice a prince; Lannes, Bessières and Marmont were all to become dukes. They had chosen of their own free will to share their General's destiny, and although four of the five were to die violently because of that decision, it is doubtful if they ever regretted their choice.

The horses of the French generals were turned loose on the beach, saddled and bridled as they were, to make their way by instinct back to Alexandria. Early the next morning, while most of the French garrison was still asleep in its tent lines, an advance post on the western outskirts of the city was startled to see these riderless horses come galloping in from the desert. The first thought of the sentries was that hostile Arabs had ambushed a detachment of the Guides; the guard was turned out; then someone recognised the mounts that belonged to Murat, Lannes, Bessières, and Marmont. The alarm was sounded and a search party was hurriedly organised to sweep the countryside to the west. The cavalry patrols had hardly left the city, however, before they met General Bonaparte's Turkish groom walking towards Alexandria, leading his master's horse by the bridle.[17] The searchers returned to the city, no doubt with mixed emotions.

Dawn came early on the 23rd of August, lighting the reaches of the Mediterranean to the north. From the mastheads of the frigates the lookouts reported that the English brig had abandoned her watch over the cove and had disappeared below the horizon. (She had in fact sailed to rejoin Sir Sidney Smith's fleet in Cyprus.) Since the wind was still fair from the south-east, the sailors were soon busy on the decks of the *Muiron* and *Carrère*, unfurling the sails and sweating at the capstans to haul up the anchors. The two faster corvettes, *Revanche* and *Fortune*, which were to act as decoys if the little convoy met the English fleet, stood out to sea.

The *Muiron's* canvas had begun to fill and her bows had already begun to swing sluggishly to the north when a small Egyptian felucca appeared from the direction of Alexandria, overhauled her, and nudged alongside. In the boat's stern-sheets, erect and proper in sober civilian dress, sat M. Percival-Grandmaison, one of the members of the Institute whom Bonaparte had brought to Egypt. With some difficulty Grandmaison climbed aboard the *Muiron*. He had learned of the General's departure only an hour or so before, when the search party had returned to Alexandria, and he had at once determined that he could not be left behind. At first Bonaparte was furious when Grandmaison begged to be taken back to France, but because Admiral Ganteaume, Bourrienne, and his fellow civilians, Monge and Berthollet, interceded for him, the General relented and allowed him to remain on board.*

By now it was full morning. The *Muiron* and *Carrère* gathered way. The blue water creamed white under their bowsprits and the tricolour flags of the Republic fluttered at their gaffs as they swept out of Marabout Bay and turned west to run along the coast up the brown North African shore.

*   *   *

With General Bonaparte aboard, there was no nautical nonsense about the admiral being absolute master of his own ship. Stronger and more determined men than Ganteaume found it natural to take second place to Bonaparte. As a rule, too, they did it willingly, even if they were as vainglorious as General Augereau or as intelligent as General Davout. Occasionally, a jealous man like General Bernadotte admitted Bonaparte's primacy grudgingly, but even Bernadotte admitted it, at least by implication. As for Admiral Ganteaume, he would not have dreamed of questioning Bonaparte's right to command, even aboard his own flagship and at sea. The Admiral had not so much as decided what course should be laid out for the voyage.

" Keep close along the coast of the Mediterranean on the African side until you get south of Sardinia," Bonaparte had told him firmly. " I have a handful of brave fellows and a few pieces of artillery. If the English appear, I will run ashore and make my

---

* This episode is based on Bourrienne's account (*Mémoires de Napoléon Bonaparte*, I, 247). A very similar story concerning a M. Blanc is told by Marmont (*Mémoires*, II, 37-9). Since Bourrienne, who was with Bonaparte on board the *Muiron,* speaks as an eyewitness, and Marmont, who was on board the *Carrère,* must have had his story at second-hand, Bourrienne's account has been preferred.

way overland to Oran, Tunis, or some other port from which we may be able to get home."[18]

The favourable south-east wind which carried the *Muiron* and *Carrère* away from Alexandria lasted only twenty-four hours.[19] It died on the morning of the second day out and the flotilla could make no further headway. This was not unexpected, since in summer the prevailing winds in the eastern Mediterranean are from the north-west. At that season of the year sailing vessels returning to France from Egypt normally tacked north to the Greek Archipelago where they could pick up variable winds and helpful westerly currents. Bonaparte, however, had decided that this route would be too hazardous. Even if the French ships did not encounter a cruising British squadron, they would certainly be sighted by merchantmen who might report their presence in European waters.[20] The General had calculated all the odds. It was automatic with him. He said that one should always look at things as though through a telescope—bringing reality close to one, but always reality.

For the next twenty-one days the *Muiron* and *Carrère* made almost no progress. Struggling against adverse winds and contrary coastal currents, the little ships were continually blown back towards the coast of Syria or in the direction of Alexandria. Sometimes at night a land breeze, arising in the east, would enable them to regain the distance lost during the day. Sometimes the whole endeavour seemed hopeless. Once, after several days' sailing, when the ships were actually off Alexandria again, it was suggested that they might as well put back into that port to await the change of wind which would come with the equinox.

The General would not hear of it. He declared that he would risk anything rather than go back. Accordingly, the four ships continued the apparently futile routine of tacking to the north-west each night only to be blown back towards the African coast the following day.

For most of those on board these idle weeks were an acute strain. The ships' quarters were hot and crowded; there were only sea-rations to eat; and any dot on the horizon might prove to be an English man-o'-war. Naturally enough, nerves became frayed and tempers grew daily shorter. Bonaparte's young generals found all this ridiculous sailing back and forth nearly intolerable. In three weeks they had covered barely twenty-four leagues. They muttered uncomplimentary things about sailors and navies and blamed poor Admiral Ganteaume—quite unjustly because he really had very little to do with it.

Although the four senior officers on the *Carrère* had absolute faith in Bonaparte, they had little use for one another. Lannes and Murat had disliked each other excessively ever since Lannes had " sold the coconut " to Bonaparte about Murat's mutinous grumblings in Egypt. Marmont felt himself superior in birth and intellect to his companions, and all three patronized Bessières, who was a colonel. Nevertheless, all in their way were remarkable men.

Joachim Murat, once a stable-boy, the third son of a Gascon innkeeper, had already made his reputation as a dashing leader of cavalry. He was a fine, swashbuckling figure of a man, big, with curly hair, and a perpetual swagger. His love for gaudy uniforms already verged on the ridiculous. He had a passion for gold braid, crimson Morocco leather riding-boots, fur-trimmed pelisses and wonderful hats surmounted with ostrich plumes and aigrettes. In Madame Junot's tart phrase, Murat " always dressed for a carnival,"[21] but although it was easy enough for the more discriminating ladies of the Parisian *salons* to laugh at Murat, no soldier who saw him at the head of the thundering squadrons of French cavalry ever forgot the sight or felt in the least like laughing.

Now, at thirty-two, Murat had been soldiering off and on for twelve years, ever since he had run away from home to join the Chasseurs of the Ardennes. Within two years he had been dismissed from the service for insubordination, and on the outbreak of the Revolution he had been earning his livelihood as a draper's assistant. Murat had found the turmoil of the years following

1789 more to his liking, but his first real chance had come on the night before 13th Vendémiaire, 1795.* That was the time General Bonaparte had stepped out of obscurity to defend the Government by clearing the streets of Paris with his " whiff of grapeshot ". Murat had been only a captain when Bonaparte had sent him galloping through the October night to bring up the forty guns of the National Guard from their park in the suburb of Sablons. He was promoted as a result of that night's work and went to Italy the following spring as Bonaparte's aide-de-camp.

*   *   *

After the Italian campaign, Murat was lucky enough to be sent to Egypt where he did brilliant work with the cavalry. He led the decisive charge at the battle of Aboukir, received a pistol wound through the lower jaw in a hand-to-hand combat, and while still in hospital was promoted general of division. It took more than a wound to suppress Murat. He wrote to his father from hospital: " The doctors tell me I shall not be in the least disfigured, so tell all the young ladies that even if Murat had lost some of his good

---

* The 13th Vendémiaire was 6th October by Gregorian reckoning. A typical extravagance of the French Revolution had been the institution of a new calendar, which would be free of all Christian connotations. The year was divided into twelve months of thirty days each, with the five extra days being taken as holidays at the end of the year. The new calendar was dated from 22nd September 1792, the day when the republic was proclaimed. For the year VIII (1799-1800) the initial days of the Revolutionary Calendar months and their Gregorian equivalents were:
1st of Vendémiaire (month of vintage)—23rd September 1799
1st of Brumaire (month of fog)—23rd October 1799
1st of Frimaire (month of frost)—22nd November 1799
1st of Nivôse (month of snow)—22nd December 1799
1st of Pluviose (month of rain)—21st January 1800
1st of Ventose (month of wind)—20th February 1800
1st of Germinal (month of buds)—22nd March 1800
1st of Floréal (month of flowers)—21st April 1800
1st of Prairial (month of meadows)—21st May 1800
1st of Messidor (month of reaping)—20th June 1800
1st of Thermidor (month of heat)—20th July 1800
1st of Fructidor (month of fruit)—19th August 1800
18th September—22nd September 1800—feast days (or *sans-culottides*).

looks, they won't find that he has lost any of his bravery in the war of love."

There was later to be a sad and ironic echo of this gallantry. But then, the Napoleonic epoch was full of echoes, many of them ironic and almost all of them somewhat sad.

On the *Carrère*, Murat had one young lady in particular in mind—Caroline Bonaparte, the General's younger sister. He had met Caroline three years earlier at Montebello and had treated her with automatic gallantry. Caroline, who had been sixteen at the time, with a beautiful, sensual face and a small high bust, had been much impressed with her cavalier. In Italy she had been no more than a passing fancy to Murat, but now times had changed. What better insurance in an uncertain world than to be the brother-in-law of General Bonaparte? Murat decided to seek Caroline out as soon as he reached France.

Jean Lannes was going back to France with quite other plans. Like Murat, whom he hated, Lannes was also a Gascon, had been a soldier for years, and had been dismissed from the Royalist army. Lannes, however, had won his reputation with the infantry. A fiery, impetuous man with a slight, wiry frame and bones of a singular toughness, Lannes at thirty was a veteran of a dozen pitched battles, and had greatly distinguished himself at Lodi, Bassano and Arcola. He had almost no formal education, being the fourth son of a peasant from the Gironde, but while Murat spent his leisure hours attempting the seduction of every pretty girl he met, Lannes spent his in the serious study of his profession. As a result, Lannes became a very good soldier indeed, but one, as Madame Junot pointed out, who " could always storm a fortress more easily than a woman ".[22]

Lannes knew the truth of this, and it made the news he had recently heard all the more bitter. He had received a musket-ball in the hip at the battle of Aboukir and had gone into the same hospital as Murat. There he had learned that his wife of four years, with whom he was still deeply in love, had just given birth to a son. Since Lannes had spent the past fourteen months in Egypt, he was now going home in a cold rage, determined on a divorce.

There was, however, some consolation. He could continue to serve under General Bonaparte, whom he looked up to as to a god.[23] Although happiness might not lie ahead, there was certain to be glory. Perhaps if Lannes could have seen how the great adventure was to end, he would have felt that his luck, after all, was no better in war than in love.

But who could possibly have foreseen what unbelievable things were lurking in the future? At the moment, Lannes did not greatly care. He leaned on his crutches by the rail, brooding on the pretty face of a Gascon girl from Perpignan.

Jean Baptiste Bessières was not a man to marry either cold-bloodedly like Murat or rashly like Lannes. In 1799, Bessières was still a bachelor, but when he chose a wife his marriage would wear well. He had been a medical student before he joined the 22nd Chasseurs in 1793, and had been no more than a good regimental officer until in Italy Bonaparte had placed him in command of the Guides, the forerunners of the Imperial Guard. Bessières was always to remain the good regimental officer, even when he was a Marshal of the Empire and the commander of the Cavalry of the Guard and the Reserve Cavalry. His men loved him and he took infinite trouble to look after their welfare.

Of all the officers on the *Muiron* and *Carrère,* Bessières was probably the least perturbed by the boredom and dangers of the voyage. A tall, handsome man of thirty-one, Bessières took life so quietly that his serenity of character was often mistaken for dullness. But Bonaparte had made no mistake in choosing Bessières to accompany him on his return from Egypt. The General had no more loyal or disinterested supporter than the big, lazy-looking man who irritated his volatile shipmates by his imperturbability.

Auguste Frederic Louis Viesse de Marmont was not imperturbable, but although he hated life on the *Carrère,* he was far too self-confident to be seriously depressed. Of his feelings at the time of embarkation he later wrote:

It would be difficult to imagine a greater joy than ours: against us were great hazards, but we were of an age when hope is lively, when one has limitless faith in the outcome. Obstacles dissolved before our eyes. Moreover, we felt that we were associated with an all-powerful destiny.[24]

In the autumn of 1799, Marmont was only twenty-five, and his many attractive qualities were no more than slightly marred by a certain secret superciliousness in his manner. The son of a minor nobleman, he had little in common with most of the newly promoted officers of the French Republic. General Bonaparte, it is true, also came from the lesser aristocracy, but that, after all, was only the Corsican aristocracy. Like Bonaparte too, Marmont was a gunner, and it had been his handling of the guns at the siege of Toulon in 1794 that had made the General single him out. In Italy Marmont had served as one of Bonaparte's aides-de-camp. The Army List of the time showed Marmont as Colonel of the Second Regiment of Horse Artillery, seconded as aide-de-camp to Lieutenant-Colonel Bonaparte, Commander-in-Chief of the Army of Italy. All his life Marmont suspected that this Army List had accurately reflected reality, that only the accidents of campaigning and the unpredictable fortunes of their professional careers placed Bonaparte ahead of him.

The four senior officers on the *Carrère* passed the time as best they could, thinking their own thoughts, dreaming their own dreams, and quarrelling among themselves. They were not politicians and most of them probably had only a very hazy idea of what might happen when they got back to Paris. They were content to leave that aspect of things to the General, and Bonaparte did not confide his plans to anyone. Meanwhile, the little ships gently pitched and rolled on the blue waters; their mastheads endlessly described slow circles in the blue sky; their old timbers creaked and groaned; and their sails crackled and flapped in the intermittent wind.

On the *Muiron*, General Berthier was unhappy.[25] As the days wore on, he was quite unable to conceal his nervous agitation and he bit the nails on his rough, red hands until they bled. He was a queer-looking little fellow at the best of times, with heavy black eyebrows and his hair combed down uncompromisingly in a fringe over his forehead. Now his shoulders drooped disconsolately and his ugly, intelligent face appeared at any moment ready to crumple into tears.

It was not so much that Berthier was a poor sailor, and it certainly was not that he lacked courage. What unmanned him was the prospect of being taken prisoner by the English. If that happened, it might be years before he got back to Paris. And in that case it was really impossible to suppose that the lovely Madame Visconti would remain faithful to him.

Love had come late to Berthier. He had been forty-four when he had first met Madame Visconti in Italy where her husband had been French ambassador to the Cisalpine Republic. Perhaps that was why he was never able to overcome his wonder at having won her. All his tour of duty in Egypt had been a torment because it had meant separation from her. During the day he had worn her portrait next to his heart and every night he had placed it by his bedside. For once in his life Berthier had even allowed his staff work to deteriorate; he had fallen ill; he had begged Bonaparte to allow him to return to France. At last, when his request had been coldly granted, he had found he could not leave his General to fight a campaign without him. Sadly he had taken out his maps and pencils, rulers and compasses again and had accompanied the Army to Syria. When he had learned of Bonaparte's plan to leave the East he had been overjoyed.

Aboard the *Muiron*, Berthier divided his days between writing a history of the Egyptian campaign and anxiously searching the sea for hostile sails. His younger comrades-in-arms declared that he spent his nights on his knees, praying before the portrait of Madame Visconti.

General Bonaparte also had troublesome personal problems, although he concealed them better than his chief-of-staff. Certainly the General looked serious and thoughtful. His secretary found him moody,[26] and he would stand for long periods on the quarterdeck with his arms behind him and his smouldering eyes fixed on the empty horizon. If Berthier wondered about Madame Visconti's fidelity, the General had no cause at all to wonder about Madame Bonaparte's. He knew. He had known, in fact, for the past fourteen months. Josephine had been unfaithful to him almost from the day of his marriage.

This, of course, was nothing unusual in revolutionary France, where the citizens and citizenesses of the Republic had freed themselves from all their chains, spiritual as well as political. The society which had recently crowned a Parisian prostitute " Goddess of Reason " before the high altar in Notre Dame was not likely to retain much regard for the outmoded morality of its priest-ridden past. Almost the first result of this emancipation had been that love was no longer secure. In Paris at least there were few who would take Josephine's infidelities very seriously.

But General Bonaparte was not a Parisian; he was a Corsican. And he had all the Corsican's inbred sense of family. This was the time-tested instinct of a race which knew that its survival depended upon it. To a Corsican, infidelity in a woman or cowardice in a man were the ultimate sins because they were the deadly ones. For centuries the Corsicans had lived too close to reality to believe that a society could tolerate them and survive.

Moreover, Bonaparte had been deeply and passionately in love with his wife. In 1796, two days after his marriage, he had set out to take command of the Army of Italy. At every post-house along the way he had written burning love letters to Josephine, sometimes as many as eight a day. He had poured out a wealth of love in those letters, tender, passionate and pristine. It was as though, out of due time, he had been miraculously granted a portion of that boyhood he had missed.

Few of his letters had been answered. While he was astounding the world with his victories in the Ligurian Hills, Josephine took a lover, a certain Hippolyte Charles, who was more polished

and personable than her "funny little Corsican" whose speech was still marked with the accent of his native island.

Not only was Josephine amoral, she was a fool as well. When Murat had been sent back to Paris to present some Austrian colours captured by the Army of Italy, his strapping figure and swaggering air caught Josephine's eye. She and Murat got along famously. On one memorable day they had a breakfast, a dinner and a supper together in the Champs Elysées, and as a souvenir of the occasion, Josephine presented Murat with a fine silver lemon-squeezer, useful in the preparation of Jamaica punch but unfortunately engraved with the Bonaparte cipher.

Not long afterwards Murat gave a champagne breakfast party to a group of hussar officers. After many bottles of champagne, Murat decided that what was needed to complete the party was Jamaica punch—a special punch he had learned to make from a charming Creole. His friends would find they had never tasted better.

" And," he added, " if I could reveal all the circumstances of that education, you would like it better still."

This was bad enough, but when Murat brought out the silver lemon-squeezer one of his companions seized it with a whoop of triumph and read aloud the name on the cipher.

That name had a sobering effect upon the party, but the story was too good for Murat's young guests to keep to themselves. Murat later claimed that the hussar officer had been too drunk to know what he was doing; the lemon-squeezer was conveniently lost; and after being the gossip of Paris for twenty-four hours, the incident was forgotten.[27] General Bonaparte heard the story, but was too much in love, and too naïve in such matters, to be convinced of the worst. Nevertheless, he was much tormented by this and other reports. He wrote warning Josephine to beware of Othello's dagger, and in another letter said: " Josephine, take care: one fine night and the doors will burst open and I shall be there."[28] But when at length he saw her again he readily accepted her version of events. Even when he discovered that Hippolyte

Charles had accompanied Josephine to Italy he allowed himself to be persuaded that his wife's friendship with that young man had been innocent. He did, however, take the precaution of having Charles cashiered and sent back to France in disgrace.

When Bonaparte had sailed for Egypt on 29th April 1798, he was still devoted to his wife. Josephine came down to the pier to see him off, and Bonaparte stood on the deck of *L'Ocean* watching her figure until it faded from sight.

However, something he heard on the voyage reawakened his suspicions. While the big warship was sailing between Malta and Alexandria, Bonaparte closely questioned some of his officers about Josephine's conduct. What he heard convinced him she had been unfaithful to him. We find him writing to his brother Joseph on 25th July 1798:

> Please look after my interests. I have great private unhappiness; the veil has at last quite fallen from my eyes . . . I have had enough of human nature. I need solitude and quiet; grandeur bores me; my emotions are dried up. Glory is stale at twenty-nine; I have used everything up; it only remains to become a real egoist.[29]

The General was to be as successful in this as in many of his more difficult endeavours. He began, as many others have done, by seeking consolation, and because of his position as Commander-in-Chief was not long in finding it.

In September, at the Tivoli Gardens in Cairo, Bonaparte met Madame Fourès, a vivacious blonde who had disguised herself in a cavalry uniform in order to go to Egypt with her bridegroom, a handsome young lieutenant in the 22nd Chasseurs. For some time, although the General showered gifts and attentions on Pauline Fourès, she remained faithful to her husband.

There was an obvious way around this difficulty. On 17th December Lieutenant Fourès was ordered back to France with despatches for the Directory. The very next evening in the Elbi-Bey Palace Bonaparte gave a dinner with Pauline as guest of honour. Towards the end of the meal the Commander-in-Chief awkwardly spilled a glass of wine on Madame Fourès' dress. Apologizing profusely, he rose and accompanied the lady into another room. The others sat waiting at the table for the pair to return. When they did not do so, the guests one by one slipped quietly away.

Unfortunately, Lieutenant Fourès returned to Egypt sooner than anticipated. The English man-o'-war *Lion*, patrolling off Alexandria, captured Fourès' ship and took the young *chasseur* prisoner. The captain of the *Lion*, who knew more of the Fourès' personal affairs than the lieutenant did himself, was most sympathetic. After all, Bonaparte had behaved very badly—not at all like a gentleman—and Admiral Nelson's officers had a strict code about such matters. If Lieutenant Fourès would only give his parole not to serve against the British again in this war, he would be put ashore so that he could straighten out his domestic troubles. Fourès gave his parole, and although Marmont tried vainly to detain him at Alexandria, he soon arrived back at Cairo in a great rage. Pauline, however, had been warned of his coming and hurriedly divorced him. When Fourès was packed off to France again, Bonaparte installed Pauline in a house adjoining the Elbi-Bey Palace. Soon the two of them were to be seen everywhere together, at reviews, banquets, and driving out in the General's carriage, often with Josephine's son, Eugene, trotting sullenly alongside.[30]

Eugene was almost alone in his disapproval. The common soldiers nicknamed Pauline " Cleopatra ", and most of the Army looked upon the liaison with envious admiration. Still, the General was not entirely happy. He wanted a child of his own, but Pauline seemed no more able to give him one than Josephine. Once he burst out angrily to a group of friends: " The silly little fool doesn't even know how to make a baby." When this was repeated to Pauline, she replied: " Who knows if I am the fool?" Bonaparte was told of the rejoinder, and his face darkened with unaccustomed self-doubt.

Now all this was in the past. Madame Fourès had been left

behind in Egypt, entrusted—rather naïvely—to Kléber's care. Josephine was in Paris, and Bonaparte had to decide what part she should play in his future. In Egypt he had threatened to divorce her. That would please his family and his pride, but it would leave him a very lonely man. Perhaps, though, he was destined to be lonely in any case . . .

The General had more than domestic worries on his mind while the *Muiron* struggled slowly west along the African coast. The political future was full of uncertainty. He had no illusions about the Government of France. The two assemblies, the Five Hundred and the Council of Ancients, were typical representative bodies of the revolutionary period, which is to say that they were fractious, vain, wordy, and incompetent. The five Directors were corrupt nonentities, but they had the power. Before now they had proved themselves vicious, cunning, and perfidious. In Egypt Bonaparte had once exclaimed: " The Directory! The Directory is composed of a set of scoundrels! They envy and hate me and would gladly let me perish here."[31]

This was probably no more than the truth. The General knew, moreover, that the civil powers had some reason to mistrust him. During the Italian campaign, he had held court like an independent sovereign, drawing up treaties and establishing republics with little pretence of consulting his Government. He had been useful to France and he resolved that France should generously return the favour. To make it easier for the French to accept him he had begun signing himself " Bonaparte " instead of " Buonaparte." In Italy he had already fixed his ambition on supreme power. On the night of the victory of Lodi, after the Austrian rearguard had been driven across the bridge and out of the town by a last brilliant attack late in the afternoon, General Bonaparte had realized for the first time that he was a prodigy and not like other men. " I felt the world flee beneath me," he said.[32] That night his vague dreams of glory had begun to crystallize into plans.

Although he confided this to no one at the time, his conduct had been enough to make the Directory suspicious. He had been the real instigator of the *coup d'état* of 18th Fructidor 1797,* when his emissary, General Augereau, had purged the moderate elements in the Directory and the Councils. On his return from Italy, Bonaparte had contemplated a further *coup* but had postponed it because " the pear was not yet ripe ".[33] It was hardly surprising that when Talleyrand had shrewdly suggested sending the General to Egypt, the Directors had accepted the idea.[34]

The politicians would have no reason to be less hostile to him now than they had been fourteen months ago. And there was also the little matter of the Army he had left behind in Egypt.

On the whole, however, it was not the Directory that Bonaparte feared. " That pack of lawyers " had been such a miserable failure as a Government that they could have little support in France. The General was more concerned about an older and more familiar enemy—time. He had better reason than his officers for impatience with the *Muiron*'s slow progress. Other men besides himself might take advantage of defeat and disaster to overthrow a weak regime. What had happened in France since that Frankfurt newspaper had been published on 6th June?

In his search for patience Bonaparte occasionally joined his officers at cards. His favourite game was *vingt-et-un,* because it was fast and because he found he could cheat at it. He had all the instincts of the great gambler, including a contempt for the rules. He cheated habitually at *vingt-et-un*—for the sheer joy of it, it must have been, since he always refused to keep his winnings at the end of the game. Sometimes, too, the General played chess, but much more rarely, for he was a third-rate player and he hated being beaten.[35]

At last, on the twenty-second day out, the wind veered around to blow strongly from the south-east. As the sails filled and the little ships picked up headway, all on board felt a lightening of the heart. For a time even Berthier forgot to bite his fingernails.

All that day the four ships drove steadily west, until at sunset

---

* 4th September 1797.

the outline of Cape Bon showed black against the scarlet sky. Here the flotilla was entering a zone of extreme danger, for a British cruiser squadron kept constant watch between Cape Bon and Marsala. However, the French vessels could not have arrived at a better time—further proof that the General did indeed possess a star. If they had reached Cape Bon earlier in the day, they would have been sighted by the English; if they had arrived a little later, they would have had difficulty in rounding the point of land by night.³⁶

As darkness fell, all lights were extinguished on the French ships. They ran on through the clear, cloudless night under full sail, the *Carrère* a little ahead of the *Muiron*. Once during the night, near the Île de Lampedouze, the *Carrère* came close to foundering when a reef suddenly loomed up only two cable-lengths ahead of her. However, the helm was swung hard to starboard and the ship glided by unharmed.³⁷

On the deck of the *Muiron* a little group had gathered around General Bonaparte. Someone voiced the question in all their minds —what would they do if the English cruisers sighted them and gave chase? Half in jest but unhesitatingly, the General answered that they would blow up the ship. At this the mathematician Monge noticeably paled and looked nervously down his huge crooked nose. Bonaparte, his eyes twinkling, turned to him and very solemnly said: " That will be *your* duty."

Towards midnight those on deck saw lights off the port bow. At first it was hoped that they might be the lamp-lit windows of some settlement on shore, but as the ships swept closer, the lights were identified as the riding-lamps of an English cruiser anchored off the coast. The officers on deck waited in nervous silence while the French vessels swung a point or two to starboard. If they were detected, the cruiser would soon overhaul them, and then they would either have to surrender ignominiously or be reduced to battered, burning hulks by the English broadsides. As the *Muiron* and *Carrère* slipped on in the darkness, the only sounds were the swish of the bow waves and the rustle and creak of sails and rigging. The period of suspense seemed very long, but within half an hour the cruiser's lights fell astern. Dawn found the French ships opposite the ancient ruins of Carthage and with the horizon clear of sail. The Cape Bon—Marsala Cordon had been safely run.

At daybreak too, Monge was found. He had not been seen on deck during the latter part of the night, but now he was discovered, still pale and with beads of sweat on his receding forehead, but with his heavy jaw set determinedly. He was waiting just outside the door of the powder-magazine.

Now the French ships turned north and, lying close to the wind, beat rapidly up the west coast of Sardinia. They still hugged the land, since Bonaparte was resolved to run ashore should they be sighted by the English. Their luck held, however; the wind remained strong and favourable; and early on 30th September they were sailing along with the blue mountains of Corsica on their right. During the morning they passed the red porphyry cliffs of the Sanguinary Isles and not long afterward weathered the headland south of Ajaccio.

Because the wind now began to back westerly, it was decided that the flotilla would put into the Gulf of Ajaccio, provided that Corsica was still held by the French. When the corvette *La Fortune* was sent ahead to reconnoitre, she met some fishing boats, and her signal flags soon brought the other three ships into the bay. There, at two o'clock in the afternoon, they dropped anchor in the roadsteads opposite the ancient citadel, above which the tricolour still flew. It had been six years since General Bonaparte had seen his native city.

*   *   *

The General's earliest memories were of this place. In his youth he had loved it with a fierce patriotism. Corsicans always found it easy to love Corsica, and the fact that they had been unable to defend its independence only made them love it the more. The Genoese had held the island as a colony until they had been driven out in 1768 by General Paoli; then the following year the French had come; and although the islanders had fought the new invaders, they had been defeated. General Paoli with some three hundred of his followers had sought refuge in England, but most Corsicans, including Napoleon's father, had come to terms with the conquerors.

There had been no reasonable alternative, but in their folksongs, the traditional consolation of the defeated, the islanders had kept alive the hopes of a national *vendetta* and had dreamed of an Avenger who would someday even the score with the French. Such legends are stronger than history. Inevitably, some were later to say that this dream had been fulfilled when Napoleon Bonaparte was born in Ajaccio on 15th August 1769.

For the first nine years of his life Napoleon had been happy in this sunlit town beside a sparkling sea. Later, when he had time to remember, he was to say: " Everything seemed better there than anywhere else." It had been a carefree life in the old, four-storey house in the Via Malerba, with his happy-go-lucky father, his loving, iron-willed mother, his brothers and sisters, his uncles and aunts and cousins. The island had been the world and the family its safe centre.

The Bonapartes had been people of consequence in Corsica, and if there had never been very much money, there had never been any great need for it. There had always been an abundance of corn and wine and oil, and although Napoleon's father had received only a small salary from the French, he always hoped that one of his interminable lawsuits would turn out well, making them all rich. Little Napoleon had taken long horseback rides on the bare uplands and through the tall pine forests. He had played boyish games among the olive trees and the mulberry groves and had spent happy days on hills fragrant with the *macchia*. He had picked the tiny June strawberries and had watched the wild bees making their bitter Corsican honey.

Suddenly in April 1779, he had been torn away from all this

and sent to the military school at Brienne in Champagne. He had been accompanied as far as Autun by his elder brother, Joseph, who was to attend the junior seminary there. Both boys were to be educated as the sons of indigent noblemen at the king's expense. When the two little boys parted at Autun, Joseph had wept, and Napoleon, at least as deeply moved, had brushed away a single tear.

Life at the Military Academy had been hard for the little Corsican boy. He had felt himself an exile in a strange land, but when he had written one despairing letter home, asking to be taken out of school, he had been told that the family could afford no other education for him. His school-fellows, the sons of French aristocrats, had spent money freely, while he never had a spare five-centime piece in his pockets. Often he could not even pay his share for a class picnic or for a class gift to one of the masters.[38] Bonaparte had reacted to humiliation with contempt, and his classmates had retaliated by laughing at his shabbiness, his accent, and his foreign ways. The happy, carefree boy from Ajaccio had grown silent, fierce, obstinate and imperious. At Brienne, for the first time, had been broken one of the threads which bound Bonaparte to humanity.

He had lived for the day when he could help liberate Corsica. Although his father had died in 1785, Bonaparte had remained resentful at his having made his peace with the French. While serving with his regiment in Valence, young Lieutenant Bonaparte had written in his notebook: "Always alone in the midst of men, I come home to dream and give myself up to the full force of my melancholy . . . If I could deliver my countrymen by destroying one man, I would go on the instant and sink the avenging blade in the tyrant's breast."[39] However, his Corsican nationalism had been mingled with certain more universal ideas. Far too intelligent to be class-conscious in the narrow sense of merely wishing to substitute one ruling clique for another, Bonaparte had nevertheless developed a hatred of all privilege which blocked the advance of merit. In his situation it was a natural philosophy to adopt. If it came to a choice between the monarchy and a republic, Bonaparte for reasons of his own favoured the republic, but he himself was neither monarchist nor republican. These were the political enthusiasms of Frenchmen.

Thus when the Revolution came, he had welcomed it—and forthwith gone back to Corsica. He felt allegiance neither to the king, whose uniform he wore, nor to the republican rabble, whom he held in contempt. But in the turbulent politics of Ajaccio he might gain control of the island.

It had not worked out that way. The Corsicans had shown their unmistakable preference for the pro-English policies of General Paoli, their national hero. After much intrigue and some fighting, Napoleon had had to go into hiding. He had sent his mother and family a message to meet him at the coast: " This country is not for us." The Bonapartes had fled to France with only what personal possessions they could carry, and Napoleon had turned his back on Corsica, wrenching its roots from his heart. From now on he was to be a wanderer and a sojourner.

This had been the second of the spiritual partings which made this man what he was.

That had been six years ago. Now on the afternoon of 30th September 1799, Napoleon Bonaparte was almost home again. But this was no sentimental journey; it was a reconnaissance; and the General was desperate for information. Shortly after the French ships had anchored off Ajaccio, a Treasury official, M. Barberi, who was a friend of the Bonaparte family, rowed out to the *Muiron*. The General asked for the newspapers and some fresh fruit and requested permission to land. M. Barberi's father was the President of the Sanitary Commission at Ajaccio, but in spite of his strong plea on the General's behalf, the other members of the Commission very rightly pointed out that the frigates had just come from Egypt where the plague was raging. Regulations were regulations, and without intending any disrespect to General Bonaparte, they were afraid he would have to observe the quarantine laws if he desired to land.

There is no direct evidence as to who conceived the solution to this impasse, but the scheme adopted has a strongly Napoleonic flavour. The President of the Sanitary Commission suggested that to soften their refusal the members of the Commission should go alongside the *Muiron* and present their compliments to the General. This they agreed to do. The coxswain of the health launch was then given orders to run into the side of the frigate so that the members of the Commission would be forced into contact with the *Muiron*'s crew. This plan was put into effect the following afternoon, and when the members of the Sanitary Commission were faced with the choice of undergoing quarantine themselves or lifting the ban on Bonaparte, they allowed the General and his suite to land.[40]

Fortunately for the Corsicans, no one in the French flotilla carried the plague.

Bonaparte's welcome was very different from the one he had been given on his previous visit. Most of Ajaccio turned out to watch him land; people flocked in from all over the island to see him; and everyone was anxious to claim acquaintance. The great man now discovered that he possessed more cousins and godchildren than he had ever believed possible.

Corsica had not changed. The valleys were still blue and aromatic with wood-smoke; stone villages still perched in militant inaccessibility on lonely crags; Monte Rotondo, where his father and mother had hidden from the French troops in 1769, still towered up over the island; swift, cold mountain streams still went clearly singing through deep gorges to the sea; the winds still smelt the same; and before the wayside shrines glowing bunches of fresh flowers still called daily on the saints for intercession. In Ajaccio itself everything also seemed the same—the same grey stone and ivory stucco houses; the same narrow cobbled streets lined with elm and plane, citron and lemon trees; goats wandered just as formerly in the back alleys; and the cathedral bells still rang out regularly over the town at angelus, vespers and compline.

But the old magic was gone. These things no longer had any power over him. Bonaparte fretted to get away. The island, which for so long had been the still centre of his spinning world, had grown too small for him.

"What will become of me," he asked Bourrienne, "if the English should learn that I have landed in Corsica? I shall be forced to stay here. That I could never endure. I have a torrent of relations pouring upon me."[41]

Bonaparte went hunting with his senior officers and their aides-de-camp in the near-by forests.[42] He visited his old home in the Via Malerba, leaned on the mantelpiece there and talked to his Corsican admirers. He gave a dinner for forty guests in the banquet-hall his prodigal father had built; the native wines were served, and Corsican pears, and stuffed wild boars, killed for the occasion by the peasants. The dinner was a great success. Marmont was gracious to everyone and Bessières quietly charming; Lannes was darkly silent; but Berthier stuttered and stammered his agreement with everything the General said; and Murat, gorgeous in his cavalry uniform, although with the wound in his jaw not yet healed, looked hungrily at the pretty Corsican girls. The evening passed in a mood of sparkling, frosty gaiety, and everyone was relieved when it was over.

The General spent some moments in the attic of the house where he used to play on rainy days and in the little summer-house on the terrace that his mother had built for him to study in. He was genuinely pleased to see his old nurse, Camilla Ilari, who embraced him and called him " *caro figlio* ". But now, as he talked with those who had known him since childhood, there was, beneath both his graciousness and their flattery, a certain reserve—

> . . . the glimmer of twilight,
> Never glad confident morning again.

This was not true of one member of his immediate family who was there to greet him. Bonaparte's Uncle Fesch, his mother's half-brother, welcomed him, not because he was a famous general and the conqueror of Italy but because he was Letizia's son. M. Fesch changed the Turkish sequins, all the money Bonaparte had brought from Egypt, for seventeen thousand French francs.[43] More important, he gave the General the latest news from France.

The affairs of the Republic had deteriorated still further since June. On 15th August General Joubert had been defeated at the battle of Novi in northern Italy. At the very outset of the battle Joubert himself had been killed, possibly by French troops.[44] Now, too, Bonaparte learned that there had been changes in the Directory. The ex-abbé Sieyès had replaced Rewbell; and with Sieyès' help the strongly republican Directors, Larevellière-Lépeaux and Merlin of Douai, had been deposed by the bloodless *coup* of the 30th Prairial.*[45] The five reigning Directors were Barras, Sieyès, Gohier, Roger-Ducos and Moulin.

Since 30th Prairial the atmosphere in Paris had been tense, and during the summer there had been a strong revival of Jacobinism. There was much bloodthirsty talk in the Café Godeau; General Jourdan, an austere and rigid Republican, had publicly toasted the resurrection of the pikes; rioting had broken out several times in the streets; and the old Jacobin Club, which had been closed when Robespierre had been hauled to execution from the Hôtel de Ville, had been reopened under the name of the *Manège*. Here Generals Jourdan, Augereau and Bernadotte formed a sort of military triumvirate among the Jacobins. General Bonaparte knew these three men well and trusted none of them.

Paris was once again apprehensive. It was afraid of a revival of the Terror, of the guillotine, of mass arrests, outlawry, and the dreaded, unanswerable charge of " incivism ". It was afraid, in short, of General Jourdan's toast, of the crowds of half-naked, bloodstained men who in 1793 had drunkenly paraded the streets with heads on pikes. Only two weeks before, in a tumultuous

---

* 18th June 1799.

assembly hall resounding with cries of " *La liberté ou la mort!*",
Jourdan had demanded that the Five Hundred declare a state of
national emergency. On this occasion Jourdan's motion had been
narrowly defeated, and Bernadotte had been hastily removed
as Minister of War, but the Jacobins would try again. As summer
faded into autumn all Paris was nervously aware that the present
lull could not last.

General Bonaparte thought it probable that the rest of France
reflected the mood of Paris. The financial situation everywhere in
the country was chaotic. For ten years incompetent demagogues
had had the ordering of affairs, and the Government would long
ago have been bankrupt if it had not been for the plunder sent back
to France by the revolutionary armies. Roads, bridges and canals
had been allowed to fall into disrepair; neglected farms and the
breakdown of the distribution system had brought the big cities
close to famine; a series of forced loans, no better than legalized
theft, had destroyed confidence and helped ruin commerce; high-
way robbery was commonplace; bands of brigands terrorized
whole districts; and in La Vendée royalist insurgents were waging
full-scale civil war.

The one thing certain was that a change was coming. Many
members of the Council of Five Hundred adhered to the extreme
Left, and none of the Directors seemed strong enough to with-
stand for long the pressure of the Parisian proletariat and the
Jacobins. Bonaparte knew the Directors; Roger-Ducos, Gohier
and Moulin were insignificant men; the ex-abbé Sieyès, who had
recently been ambassador at Berlin, was crafty and unscrupulous
but timid; and Barras, who had played a courageous part in the
overthrow of Robespierre, had degenerated to the point where
all that he did was marked by a deep, corrupt fatigue. Moreover,
the General had a private reason for disliking Barras—Josephine,
not so many years ago, had been Barras' mistress.

For the time being, however, some sort of political equilibrium
was still maintained. Late in July, Fouché, the Minister of Police,
had closed the *Manège*, suppressed eleven Jacobin and royalist

newspapers, seized the presses and arrested the editors.[46] Bonaparte wondered about Fouché. He had been one of those who had
voted for the death of the king, and as the Revolution's representative at Lyons he had gained a terrible reputation for bloodthirsty ferocity. The butcher of Lyons, people called him. He was
utterly untrustworthy, profligate, energetic and restless, but he
was an admirable Minister of Police.

Talleyrand, who not so long ago had been His Grace the
Bishop of Autun, was also in Paris—intriguing, of course, and
probably with Fouché. Bonaparte had reason to be angry with
Talleyrand, because he had broken his promise to go to Turkey
as French ambassador, at a time when the General had badly
needed a skilled diplomat with the Porte. But that had been a
year ago. Now it would be best to wait and see.

All in all, the situation in France was more favourable than
Bonaparte had thought, but for this very reason he was doubly
anxious to reach Paris. The thought of being detained in the
lazaretto of Toulon tormented him, and he worried about the
many enemies he had in the capital.[47] How much longer would
the Jacobins tolerate the shift to the Right that had been achieved
on 30th Prairial? On that day the Jacobin generals Jourdan and
Bernadotte had looked on contemptuously at the riotous Councils.

Jourdan had said: " If I wanted to, I could put an end to all
that with twenty grenadiers."

And Bernadotte had replied: " Twenty grenadiers is too much.
Four men and a corporal are quite enough to clear out the
lawyers."

If this wind did not change soon, Bonaparte feared he might
arrive in Paris only to find that a Government of Public Safety
had been established by Bernadotte.

Before landing in Corsica, the General had toyed with the
idea of going directly to Italy to take command of the army there,
but now he said to Marmont: " When the house is crumbling, is
it the time to busy oneself in the garden?" Bonaparte purchased a
large launch at Ajaccio and hired twelve of the best Corsican

sailors as a crew. The launch was to be towed behind the *Muiron*
so that, if the frigate were overhauled by the English fleet, he
could jump into the boat and make for shore.[48]

On the evening of 6th October, Ajaccio gave a ball to honour
General Bonaparte. Most of the French officers attended, but the
affair was soon interrupted by a message from Admiral Ganteaume. The wind had at last veered to the south, and not a
moment was to be lost if the flotilla was to make the French
coast. After hasty farewells, everyone hurried down to the water-
front and embarked, each in his ball costume. A few minutes later
the four French ships were leaving the Bay of Ajaccio.[49].

Bonaparte was never to set foot in Corsica again.

*   *   *

The first day's voyage was uneventful, but just at sunset on the
second day, when the Îles d'Hyères south of Toulon could
already be dimly discerned on the horizon, the lookout on the
Muiron announced that fourteen English men-o'-war lay dead
ahead. Bonaparte held a hurried consultation with Admiral Ganteaume. The admiral was unnerved by the appearance of such an
overwhelming enemy force and his fears were plainly reflected
on his tremulous face. He suggested that the only thing to do
was to turn about and run before the enemy back to Corsica.

The General stood for a moment or two deep in thought. The
English and French ships were closing fairly rapidly, but the
French still had some slight advantages. While the English men-
o'-war were plainly visible, outlined blackly against the crimson
western sky, the French vessels, lying to the east and partially
concealed by a light haze, would be much harder to distinguish.[50]
If they continued on their course, closing with the English fleet,
it would probably be some time before they were recognized as
French. Before then it might be dark. Moreover, the coast of
France was very near. This adventurous crossing from Egypt had
already taken forty-six days. France was now only a matter of

hours away. If the worst happened, there was always the launch and the twelve picked Corsican sailors. Bonaparte made up his mind. The great gambler, who was to gamble so often in the years ahead—at Marengo, and Aspern-Essling, and Moscow, and Waterloo—took what was perhaps the greatest gamble of his career.

" No! " he said imperiously. " Spread all sail. Every man to his post. To the north-west! "

Ganteaume, although in a pitiful state of agitation, obeyed without question. The French ships continued on their course, drawing nearer and nearer to the enemy. Everyone on board except the General betrayed the most lively alarm. They were risking everything on a colossal bluff and on the hope that night would overtake them before the English men-o'-war. Bonaparte was too busy to be agitated. A series of brisk orders were barked out; the twelve Corsican sailors were to stand by ready to take to the launch; a number of officers were told off to accompany Bonaparte should he decide to abandon the *Muiron;* his secretary was given detailed instructions as to the disposal of various important papers.[51]

No one slept that night on the *Muiron*. The sun went down while the English ships were still some distance away and the French flotilla then swung a little to starboard, making for Nice instead of Toulon. The French officers waited anxiously on the darkened decks, watching the signal flares and listening to the signal guns of the searching English squadron. Everyone's nerves were kept on edge for several hours, but after midnight the tension began to ease somewhat as the sound of the enemy's cannon could be heard further and further to the left. Finally the intermittent booming died away and the sea lay empty and silent.

With the morning the French coast was close at hand and there was no sign of the fourteen English men-o'-war. The bluff had succeeded.

Was it luck alone that made it succeed? Historians hostile to Napoleon have usually claimed that it was, but such claims are

singularly unconvincing. The testimony of General Savary on this
point is interesting. Savary wrote:

> I have met officers of the English navy who assured me that the
> two frigates had been seen, but were considered by the [English]
> Admiral to belong to his squadron, since they steered their course
> towards him, and as he knew we had only one frigate in the
> Mediterranean and one in Toulon harbour, he was far from sup-
> posing that the frigates he had sighted could have General Bona-
> parte on board.[52]

If this was luck, the word must be taken to mean much more
than blind chance. General Bonaparte knew better. In later years,
when he was considering the promotion of a general officer, the
first question he usually asked was: " Is he lucky?" And this was
not superstition, but instinct. Fortune does not favour the brave.
She favours the courageously intelligent.

*   *   *

At first the French were uncertain as to where on the coast
they had made their landfall, but as they sailed closer in they
recognised the Bay of Fréjus in Provence. At eight o'clock on the
morning of 9th October the four ships dropped anchor in the
roadstead off the little village of Saint-Raphaël. The Corsican
launch was at last put to use when it was sent ashore to inform
the Fréjus port authorities of the flotilla's arrival. Within the hour
the Bay of Fréjus was swarming with small boats, all converging
on the *Muiron* to greet General Bonaparte.

At Ajaccio the quarantine regulations had delayed the General's
debarkation for a day. At Saint-Raphaël, where the Bonapartes
were not so well known, the threat of the plague was immediately
waved aside. The people of France, who in the past ten years
had suffered so much in the name of the Revolution, were desperate for a deliverer. The General and his staff landed amid a
cheering crowd. When some French officers warned the people

that their enthusiasm might be exposing them to the plague, they were told: " We prefer the plague to the Austrians! "

Shortly afterwards Bonaparte set out in a post-chaise on the Paris road, accompanied by Berthier and Bourrienne. Murat, Marmont, Lannes and Admiral Ganteaume decided to go to Toulon to pick up carriages. Bessières seems to have made his own arrangements; most probably, considering the character of the man, he was busy seeing to the comfort of his Guides. These unfortunate soldiers were the only ones forced to obey the quarantine laws; they spent the next thirty days in the lazaretto at Toulon.

That evening the admiral and his three companions stopped for the night in an inn at Vitauban, but in the small hours of the morning they were awakened by the rumble of fast-driven carriage wheels on the cobbled street outside. Later they learned that the carriages had belonged to the health officials from Toulon, hurrying to Fréjus to quarantine the ships.[53]

Bonaparte spent the first night at Aix. He had been escorted all the way there by cheering crowds and, as darkness fell, by relays of men with torches who ran alongside his post-chaise. At Aix the General received a copy of a letter written to him by the Directory the previous June. This letter had authorized him to return to France, although it had specified that he bring his army with him. That important qualifier had not been complied with, but the Directors' order would nevertheless prove useful. If it became necessary to confuse public opinion on the subject of the deserted army, it would now be possible to say that he had been ordered back to France—a half truth, but a convenient one. Bonaparte sat down and wrote to the Directory, informing them of his landing and saying:

At the end of several diplomatic conferences I obtained the English newspapers up to 6th June wherein I learned of the defeats of Jourdan in Germany and Schérer in Italy. I left at once with the frigates *Muiron* and *Carrère,* although they are slow sailers. I

thought it right to ignore the dangers, for I had to place myself
where my presence could be useful. In this belief I would have
wrapped myself in my cloak and left in an open boat if I had not
had the frigates . . . I should be in Paris almost as soon as this
letter, but the dry and cold air here affects and tires me, and that
will delay me for thirty or forty hours.[54]

The news of the General's arrival everywhere evoked the live-
liest enthusiasm among the people of Provence. The roadsides
were lined with men and women who shouted " *Vive Bonaparte!* "
Pretty girls dressed in the tricolour threw flowers at the carriage.
Houses and inns along the route were decked out in flags and
ribbons. At Lyons, which he reached on 11th October, his carriage could scarcely make its way through the city, so dense were
the crowds. The city was gay with coloured lanterns; people
danced in the streets; a magnificent firework display was held
that evening; and the General went to the Celestine Theatre to
attend a performance entitled " The Return of The Hero " which
had been hastily prepared in his honour.

At Lyons some of his young officers caught up with him. When
Bonaparte paid a call on General de Marbot, who happened to be
passing through the town, Murat and Lannes at least were in
attendance. They stayed in the parlour of the hotel suite, making
conversation with de Marbot's young son, while Bonaparte and
the elder de Marbot were closeted together for an hour in the
bedroom. Young de Marbot was thrilled to find himself in such
dashing company, and was fascinated by the officers' bronzed
faces, by their Turkish sabres slung by cords, and by their tales
of campaigning in Egypt. He was particularly attracted to
General Lannes, who forgot his private grief long enough to be
extremely gracious to the boy.

The next day when General de Marbot tried to continue his
journey—he was on his way to assume a divisional command in
the Army of Italy—he found that all the post-horses in Lyons
had been commandeered for General Bonaparte to make an
inspection of some nearby military installation. De Marbot took

the inconvenience calmly, but remarked: " This is the beginning of omnipotence."[55]

After breaking his journey at Lyons, Bonaparte hired a fast, light carriage to take him to Paris. The shortest way from Lyons to the capital was through Burgundy, but at the last minute the General decided to take the more roundabout road through Bourbonnais. Later he was to develop a habit of suddenly changing his route or his time of departure,[56] probably for the same reason which influenced him at Lyons. He knew that word of his landing at Fréjus had already been signalled to Paris by field semaphore and he suspected that some of his enemies might send an assassin to intercept him. On this occasion, the sudden change of plan was to have a quite unforeseen consequence.

The General travelled hard and fast to Paris. It was six o'clock on the cold, grey morning of 16th October when his carriage drew up in front of his home in the Rue de la Victoire and Bonaparte got out, stiff and weary from his journey. The door of the house opened and there on the threshold to welcome him stood his mother.

As soon as the General saw Madame Letizia rather than Josephine waiting to greet him, he knew that something was wrong. Seized by sudden apprehension, he ran nimbly up the stone steps of his front porch to where his mother stood, very straight and unsmiling, her lips firmly together and her glowing black eyes fixed on his. Bonaparte's first thought was that his wife might be ill, but when he asked Letizia she shook her head in silence. Still without speaking, she stood to one side to let him enter and then closed the heavy oak door behind him.

PART TWO

Intrigue in Paris

ON 13th October, the same day that Bonaparte had set out from Lyons on the Bourbonnais road, Gohier gave a dinner party in his apartments at the Luxembourg. Dinner parties were held almost every night at the Luxembourg, although food was scarce in the crowded tenements and shabby houses where most of the six hundred thousand inhabitants of Paris lived. Now that the Revolution was ten years old, not much was heard from the leading republicans about Spartan simplicity and the evils of luxury. The politicians and their friends dressed well, dined well, wined well, and were already beginning to ape the old royalist manners —a far cry from the days of 1793 when it had been considered not quite democratic to wash or wear clean linen. Gohier's dinner party was as fashionable and glittering as any of the *ancien régime,* but there was more than a suggestion of the *demi-monde* about it.

Gohier had been President of the Directory since the previous June. He liked being President, and his self-satisfaction was reflected in his heavy, pompous face. His high office, of course, was no more than he deserved. Although there had been some terrible times in the past ten years, Gohier had never faltered, never compromised his principles. When Louis XVI had been tried in the National Convention, Gohier had been one of the three hundred and sixty-one deputies who had voted for " *la mort* ", and he had been Minister of Justice during the Terror. Some people, he knew, called him " the casuist of the guillotine ", but Gohier, secure in the knowledge of his own rectitude, ignored such whisperings. Now, at the age of fifty-nine, he felt that his talents had at last been adequately recognized. Tonight, as had become his habit of late, he hovered about Madame Josephine Bonaparte, like an elderly and uncertain hawk who remembered the taste of chicken but had forgotten how to strike.

Most of those at Gohier's this evening belonged to the clique which Bonaparte was shortly to nickname the Decadents. The chief Decadent was the Director Barras who was there with his mistress of the moment, Madame Sainte-Aubin, a blonde actress from the Theatre Feydeau. Many of Barras' female friends were actresses, or called themselves by that title. Barras, who had once been a viscount and a soldier, had turned revolutionary and ter-rorist after the storming of the Bastille. On three brief occasions since 1789 he had been virtually military dictator of France— on 9th Thermidor 1794, when Robespierre had been arrested; on 13th Vendémiaire 1795, when General Bonaparte had defended the Tuileries; and on 18th Fructidor 1796, when Augereau's *coup* had purged the Directory and Councils.*

In spite of his revolutionary past, there was no niggling repub-lican austerity about Barras. He contrived, so Marmont said, to combine the vices of the new order with those of the old.[1] He dressed richly—he was the only one of the Directors who could wear with elegance the official costume designed by David, with its scarlet cloak and plumed hat—and not so long ago he had been ambitious for both power and money. Now, from weari-ness, he was ambitious only for money. Yet although his dis-solute life had left its mark upon him, Barras undoubtedly still had a presence. He swaggered about " like a master-at-arms,"[2] and when he spoke his clear, bell-like tones were incongruously sweet. However, no one was any longer taken in by his pose of being the strong man of the Republic. Strange stories circulated about

---

* 27th July, 6th October, and 4th September.

him and his château at Grosbois where he surrounded himself with women and a few male hangers-on who were for the most part shady financiers and profiteering government contractors.

Talleyrand was also at Gohier's this evening, leaning on his ebony cane and smiling at everyone. The former bishop of Autun smiled a great deal. General Lannes, who neither liked nor understood Talleyrand, once said that if, when you were talking to him, someone was to come up behind him and kick him sharply, you would never be able to tell it from his face.[3]

By now, at one time or another, Talleyrand had been a supporter of almost every political party in France. Born an aristocrat, he had been prevented from becoming a soldier by an accident in childhood which had left him lame. Perhaps his lameness had warped his character or perhaps he had been born to take vengeance on the world. At all events, although he was without faith or ethical principle, he had entered the Church, and because of his ancient name the king had made him a bishop. Talleyrand had been a Freemason and an atheist, but he had represented the religious of Autun in the Constituent Assembly of 1789 and the following year had strongly supported the Civil Constitution of the Clergy. At the Feast of Pikes on 14th July 1791, in the Champ de Mars, Talleyrand had sung the first mass of the new state religion and had laid his soft white hands on the first national bishops to be consecrated in defiance of the Pope. This task done, Talleyrand had been content to leave the care of souls to his new creatures, and when heads had begun to fall into the sawdust basket, he had cautiously solicited a diplomatic appointment in London. When the British expelled him, he had gone to the United States, and when the Americans had expelled him, he had gone to Germany. He had come back to France in the quieter atmosphere of 1796 and had for a time been Minister of Foreign Affairs. Now, for some reason, no one any longer trusted him and he was out of office, living quietly with the divorcée, Madame de Grande, and intriguing with every man and woman of influence in Paris.

Talleyrand was one of the few people in Gohier's *salon* who had been born into such luxury, yet he was the most plainly dressed man there, staid and quietly conservative in his black suit and white linen. That, at least, was apt to be one's first impression. Later perhaps, when there was time for second thoughts, this mental image was inclined to blur somewhat, to be edged with doubt, almost with uneasiness. The black suit had been so richly, exotically black; the smooth, bland face with its broad forehead and mobile mouth had been too consistently smooth and bland; the charming smile had remained in place too long; the air of self-possession, which at first had been merely soothing, in retrospect seemed somehow unnatural, almost Satanic . . . And once the thought came, it could not quite be exorcised. No one any longer believed in such fancies, of course. Nor in the Principal involved. Yet if there had been a Devil, and if men could have made pacts with him . . . Almost everyone was a little afraid of Talleyrand.

Most of Gohier's guests were only on the fringe of politics. Concern for the fate of the Republic was not what formed their common bond. The old actor, Talma, was there, with his handsome mistress Julie Carreau. But by far the most striking woman in this strange clique was Therizia Tallien, a famous actress who had once been Barras' mistress. The tall, magnificently proportioned Madame Tallien still moved with assurance through all the fashionable Parisian *salons*. Generally, as tonight, her raven-black hair was set off by an exquisite Cashmere shawl of brilliant red, and wherever she went she was the centre of male attention. But Therizia no longer presided over Barras' town house—and this was certainly a symptom, and might even be a cause, of Barras' decline.

After dinner, several card tables were set up in Gohier's suite for loo, whist and *vingt-et-un*, but Madame Josephine Bonaparte preferred to play " hazard ", a dice game played on a large table covered with green baize. Tonight as she stood by the table, watching the fall of the dice, the slight flush of excitement on her

face made her appear younger than her actual age of thirty-seven.
Those who disliked Josephine claimed that she spent hours in front
of her mirror repairing her faded beauty and that she displayed
a distinct preference for candlelight. But it was mostly other
women who said so, and even they could not entirely deny her
charms. Madame Junot, for instance, wrote that she "was still a
fine woman; her teeth, it is true, were already frightfully
decayed, but when her mouth was closed, she looked, especially
at a little distance, both young and pretty."[4]

Few men were so qualified in their praise. They admired her
supple, elegant movements, her natural grace, and the soft Creole
abandonment of her gestures. Years later one man who had known
her well wrote: "In pleasure, as in grief, she was beautiful, and
even against your will you would smile when she smiled; if she
was sad, you would be also." He remembered too how pleasant
had been the tones of her voice, "so sweet that the servants would
stop suddenly in the halls to listen to it."[5] Josephine's reputation
has suffered unduly because the admirers of Napoleon have found
it convenient to blacken her. She had faults enough to be sure,
but she also possessed gaiety and goodness of heart. She loved
jewels, flowers, paintings, music and laughter, and what influence
she had with her husband was invariably used for merciful ends.[6]
In the years to come a large number of people were to owe their
lives and freedom to Josephine's intercession. However, there was
a strongly sensual streak in her character, and at this period of
her life she still took lovers. It was even said that she was
Gohier's mistress, although in this people were almost certainly
mistaking the elderly President's dreams for reality.

Just before midnight Fouché entered the *salon*. He was a
pallid man of medium height, with high cheekbones and a small,
thin-lipped mouth, but the most extraordinary feature about
him, the thing that made most people instinctively shrink away,
was his terrible blank stare, as though he had two glass eyes.
Like Talleyrand and Sieyès, Fouché was an apostate cleric, but
he had not developed that frightful look during the twenty years

he had taught science in the oratories of Nantes and Paris. Perhaps it was a legacy from the five months he had spent at Lyons between November 1793 and March 1794, when the guillotines and firing squads under his command had killed nearly two thousand people.

Fouché stood for a moment by the door, looking about him with his sightless gaze, then walked quickly to Josephine's side.

These two knew each other well. The first thing Fouché had done on becoming Minister of Police in August had been to establish a system of informers who would keep him in touch with the intrigues of Paris. The money for this he found by levying an unofficial " tax " on the gambling houses and brothels of the capital. At Barras' suggestion, Fouché had approached Josephine and offered to provide her with money from these secret funds in return for any interesting information she happened to come across. To seal the bargain Fouché with his own hands had given Josephine an initial gift of one thousand louis. Josephine had been grateful for the money and had earned every sou of it, for, as Fouché said, " she saw all Paris ".[7] Now Fouché in turn, had some information for Josephine.

Drawing her to one side, he told her that her husband had landed at Fréjus and was on his way to the capital. Josephine paled at Fouché's news and for a moment her consternation was plainly visible. There was good reason for her alarm. For nearly a year she had had no word from the General, and she had been too busy enjoying herself to care, but she knew that Joseph and Lucien Bonaparte had kept their brother informed of her escapades. She at once left the gaming table and sought out her host.

Fouché watched her go without the least flicker of speculation appearing on his face.

Like Josephine herself, Gohier seemed to feel more astonishment than joy on hearing of General Bonaparte's return. The President did not trouble to hide his feelings, but Josephine was already slipping back into the role of dutiful wife. She said:

"President, you must not believe that Bonaparte has come with any designs against liberty. And when he hears that I have been associating so much with you and have been received into your house, he will be flattered and pleased."

Then to Madame Gohier she added: "I am going to meet him. It is important to me that I see him before his brothers who have always detested me. As for the rest, I have nothing to fear from their calumnies."

Josephine left, and the long *salon* at once began to buzz with the news of Bonaparte's arrival. Talleyrand smiled blandly and said:

"How pleasant it is to see a wife of three years so eager to greet her husband."

*   *   *

The same evening that Gohier was host to the Decadents, the Director Sieyès was also giving a dinner party in his suite in the Luxembourg. The ex-abbé was a dry, taciturn man with a prematurely old face, criss-crossed with innumerable small wrinkles. In 1789 he had become famous overnight as the author of the revolutionary pamphlet *What Is The Third Estate?* However, he had never been able to repeat this first literary success and as the Revolution grew fiercer his admirers had discovered that he was obscure in debate and timid in action. Nevertheless, by silence and good luck, rather than by any positive accomplishment, Sieyès had obtained a reputation for profundity, and since abandoning Holy Orders he had acquired a considerable amount of money. Sieyès had almost as high a regard for money as for his own safety. When he was asked what he had done during the Terror, Sieyès used to reply: "*J'ai vécu*—I survived." The phrase would have served as a concise summary of his whole life.

Sieyès' dinner party was very different from Gohier's. His guests, who were all men, were not chiefly interested in the pursuit of pleasure, but were united in their detestation of the

Government. Some of them, like Sieyès himself, were intriguers who hoped to profit from any change; some were idealists and patriots sickened by the misfortunes of France; but none of them were of sufficient stature to control the drift of events. The great revolutionaries, who might have played the part of a Cato for the French Republic, were dead. Mirabeau's dissolute life had killed him before his time; the horrible Marat had been stabbed in his bath by Charlotte Corday; and Danton, Roland, Robespierre and St Just had all been guillotined when the Revolution had turned to devour its children. Of the gigantic figures of the early years only Carnot had escaped, and he was in exile in Switzerland. None of the lesser men who remained could prevent the accession of a Caesar.

Almost all of them would have done so if they could, for those who grouped themselves around Sieyès were essentially moderates who hoped for a stable, bourgeois republic. They were afraid both of the Jacobins and the royalists. Sieyès himself, however, was said to favour a limited monarchy, for he had read that the English had one and he admired what he thought was the English system.

For weeks now Sieyès had been plotting to overthrow the Directory and the Constitution of the Year III. Sieyès had a new constitution for France. He carried it with him everywhere in his pocket, although he never showed it to anyone. Sieyès was proud of his constitution. He had, after all, drafted it himself. Only one thing thwarted the realization of his ambition—he lacked the military force to overthrow the Government. Consequently he looked about him for a sword. For a time it had appeared that General Joubert might be the soldier he required, and if Joubert could have won a victory in Italy, Sieyès had planned to bring him back to Paris with his glory fresh upon him and use him as the military leader of a *coup d'état*. Unfortunately, Joubert had been ill-advised enough to get himself killed at the Battle of Novi. Worse still, Sieyès could not quite be sure whether Joubert had been killed by the enemy or assassinated by someone who guessed the plot. By the middle of October, therefore, although Sieyès maintained an uneasy alliance with Barras in the Directory and could count on a solid block of votes in the Council of Ancients, his position was growing daily more desperate.

The Jacobins had made one attempt to seize power that summer when General Jourdan had plotted with Bernadotte, the Minister of War, to arrest Sieyès and Barras and form a new Committee of Public Safety. Somehow Sieyès had learned of this conspiracy, and for a time had been very much afraid. Whenever Bernadotte had come before the Directory Sieyès had hissed in an audible aside: " *Voilà Catalina!* " But as one of his many enemies unkindly said, Bernadotte, who looked like an eagle, was really a goose. He had cautiously declined to take any positive action, and Sieyès had managed to oust him from his Ministry, replacing him with Dubois de Crancé, who was a good republican but no Jacobin. At Fouché's instigation, the strongly republican General de Marbot had been replaced as commandant of Paris by old General Lefèbvre, who was no more than an " illustrious sergeant ".[8] Largely through the efforts of Lucien Bonaparte, Jourdan's attempt to have the Council of Five Hundred declare a state of national emergency had been defeated. Lucien had risen in the Assembly and declared: " There is not one of us here who would not be ready to stab with a poniard the first man who dared to set himself up as dictator of France."[9]

Lucien liked to make public reference to poniards.

After the defeat of Jourdan's motion there had been a period of uneasy quiet while the Jacobin and royalist parties in the Assembly each sought military support to overthrow the other and each declared passionately that it was doing no such thing. Sieyès had then approached General Moreau, who had good-naturedly agreed that something should be done, but who seemed in no hurry to do it. Moreau had no love for the Jacobins— his father had been guillotined—but he was not a politician and he had little initiative.

Towards the end of September the political tension had lessened somewhat when the fortunes of France unexpectedly took a turn for the better. In Holland, General Brune had defeated the Duke of York's army; in Switzerland, in a brilliant two-week campaign known as the battle of Zurich, General Masséna had heavily repulsed Korsakov; and the other Russian general, Suvarov, had been forced to make a desperate retreat through the Alps. The ring of enemies closing in on France had been broken, but none of those who wanted a change of government were entirely pleased by the success of their country's arms.

Among the guests at Sieyès' dinner party on 13th October were General Moreau, the reluctant conspirator, and Lucien Bonaparte, who was as enthusiastic in conspiracy as he was in everything else. When word was brought in half way through the meal that General Bonaparte had landed in France, a sudden silence fell at the table. Baudin, the deputy from the Ardennes to the Council of Ancients, was overjoyed. He saw the General in exactly the same light as the cheering crowds at Fréjus, Aix and Lyons. At last France had a saviour. Poor Baudin was so overcome with delight that later that night he had a heart attack and died, thus becoming the first victim of the hero's return.

Sieyès, when he heard the news, drew down the corners of his mouth and said: " He is too late."

Moreau was relieved. He turned to Sieyès and said: " There is your man. He will manage your *coup d'état* much better than I should."

Lucien Bonaparte said nothing at all.

* * *

The next day the five Directors met at the Luxembourg to debate what they should do about their disobedient General. By now they knew that Bonaparte was being acclaimed everywhere along his route. They may even have heard of the orator in the

Midi who had declaimed: " Go, General, and defeat the enemy, and we will make you king."[10]

Here at last would seem to be a problem upon which the Directors could agree. The General might be a threat to all of them, for it was not impossible that he would sweep into power at once on the crest of his popularity and that the despised government, the representative assemblies and the Republic itself would be washed away in the undertow. Bonaparte could certainly do this if he wished. He had the people on his side and enough of the army. The only question was whether he had also the will to become a tyrant.

By the terms of the Constitution the Directors were officially tied together, like men in a three-legged race, and nothing could be done in France until a quorum of at least three of them had agreed to it, but they were suspicious of each other, quick to look to their individual advantage, and well aware that they had no support in the country. The Directors represented no one but themselves, but they could not work easily together even when their own interests were at stake. On 14th October their discussion was marked by the usual discord.

Sieyès, it was true, was still in search of a sword, but Bonaparte's sword was a little too long to please the ex-abbé.[11] Barras, who was easily frightened these days, was frankly apprehensive, but could not make up his mind what to do. Gohier, who was so fond of Josephine, disliked her husband and felt towards him all the angry jealousy that a vain nonentity feels towards a natural superior. Roger-Ducos and Moulin, as was their custom, took their cue from Sieyès and Gohier respectively, and when Sieyès and Gohier were undecided they were undecided too.

Theoretically at least, the problem facing the Directors was a simple one, and when they called in Boulay de La Meurthe, the President of the Five Hundred, he put it to them in simple terms. Here was a general of the Republic who had abandoned a French army without orders. Moreover, this general had broken the quarantine laws at Fréjus.

" *Eh bien*," said Boulay de La Meurthe, " I'll take it upon myself to denounce him tomorrow from the tribune and have him outlawed."

Sieyès protested that, if this were done, Bonaparte would have to be shot.

Boulay de La Meurthe shrugged. " Those details don't concern me," he said grandly. " If we outlaw him, he can then be guillotined, shot or hanged. The method of execution doesn't matter."[12]

The Directors declined to take so uncomplicated a view. They did not feel up to a trial of strength with General Bonaparte, and perhaps, too, they suspected Boulay de La Meurthe's sincerity. He might, after all, be merely one more man who wanted to overthrow the Government. If so, he might believe that the easiest way to accomplish this would be to encourage the Directory to arrest Bonaparte. Sieyès, Gohier, and Barras eyed each other doubtfully, each wondering what the other was really thinking. Finally the Directors sent a brief message to the Council of Five Hundred. At the end of a routine military report they appended a postscript which stated, almost as an afterthought:

> The Directory announces with pleasure to the Council that General Berthier has disembarked on the 17th [Vendémiaire] at Saint-Raphaël with Bonaparte.

A depressing financial debate was in progress in the Five Hundred. A budget deficit of some four hundred million francs had been revealed, and no one had any idea where more money could be raised. The forced loan had realised less than a third of the revenue anticipated and it had brought the nation's commerce almost to a standstill. The deputies were glad enough to interrupt their deliberations while the bulletin was read.

The Directors' announcement, with its ridiculous inversion of names, threw the Council into an uproar. The deputies leapt to their feet, cheering and waving their hands. Many of them, like the people they represented, associated Bonaparte with the two things the nation desperately longed for—victory and peace. A dozen fervent speeches were made, all praising the General and prophesying that he would bring fresh glory to France. The legislative band struck up a patriotic tune, and no more work was done for the remainder of the sitting.

By evening Paris had heard the news, and Paris reacted just as Lyons had done. Strangers stopped each other on the street to pass the good word along; theatre performances were interrupted while the bulletin was read to the audiences; new songs in honour of Bonaparte were hastily composed and sung; special editions of *le Messager* and *le Rédacteur* appeared on the streets, and the newsboys cried out: "Bonaparte in France, Landing at Saint-Raphaël *il est arrivé!*"; regimental bands marched through the city, pounding out *La Marseillaise* and *Ça ira*.

The Directors listened to all this sourly, but they were at least glad that they had not followed Boulay de La Meurthe's advice.

*   *   *

Josephine had already left Paris. She had departed by carriage early in the morning, without an escort and with no other servants than the postillion. Her sixteen-year-old daughter, Hortense, accompanied her, and at the last minute young Louis Bonaparte, the only one of her husband's family with whom she was still on friendly terms, decided that his brother's wife could not travel through France completely unprotected and so came along in his own carriage. Josephine counted on meeting Bonaparte somewhere along the Burgundy road between Paris and Lyons.[13]

As she had confessed to Madame Gohier the previous evening, Josephine was a little anxious. Although the possibility that her husband might suddenly return had occasionally nagged at the back of her consciousness, she never worried about the future before it became necessary to do so. There was something very childlike about Josephine's mind, but she seldom found this a handicap. The General, for instance, did not love her for her mind.

Napoleon in the Council of 500 at St Cloud, 1799

Joachim Murat (1767–1815), Cavalry commander and Marshal of the Empire, created King of Naples by Napoleon in 1808 (*Gérard*)

Caroline Murat (1782–1839), sister of Napoleon, wife of Joachim Murat, and Queen of Naples (*Gérard*)

Jean-Baptiste Bessières (1766–1813), Marshal of the Empire, Duke of Istria, killed in action at Rippach

Louis Alexandre Berthier (1753–1815), Marshal of the Empire, Prince of Neuchâtel and Wagram. Chief of Staff throughout most of the Napoleonic epoch, committed suicide at Bamberg.

Jean-Baptiste Jourdan (1762–1833), Marshal of the Empire and Chief of Staff to King Joseph in Spain

Paul, Vicomte de Barras (1755–1829)

Pierre François Charles Augereau (1757–1816), Marshal of the Empire and Duke of Castiglione

Charles Maurice de Talleyrand-Périgord (1754–1838), Prince of Benavente, served Napoleon as Foreign Minister until 1808 and was instrumental in restoring the Bourbons in 1814.

Auguste Frédéric Louis de Marmont (1774–1852), Marshal of the Empire, Duke of Ragusa and Napoleon's oldest friend, betrayed the Emperor 1814 and died in Vienna in exile.

Now, on the road to Lyons, Josephine felt no more than vaguely apprehensive. She was sure that if she could only reach Napoleon before Joseph or Lucien got to him, everything would be all right, just as everything had been all right in Italy three years ago. She had heard rumours about her husband and Madame Fourés in Egypt, and of course she had believed them, but the time had not yet come when Josephine felt any fear of a rival.

The worst of it was that she had quarrelled seriously with her husband's family. That Corsican clan, headed by Madame Letizia Bonaparte, would have been a formidable group for any new daughter-in-law to face. Letizia's piercing black eyes and natural dignity had made Josephine uncomfortable from the first, and the rest of the family had been even worse. The General had four brothers—Joseph, Lucien, Louis and Jerome—and three sisters —Elisa, Pauline and Caroline. All bore a strong resemblance to each other, both in physical characteristics and in temperament. They quarrelled continually among themselves, but turned a united front to any interloper who seemed to threaten what they regarded as their interests. To the Bonapartes Napoleon was a family asset like inherited wealth, and they were quick to draw up their own laws of entail. They had resented Josephine from the beginning, the more so because she had brought to her marriage two children whom the General treated as though they were his own. At first the family had been polite enough, although it had been a watchful politeness. Letizia had even written Josephine a friendly letter of welcome, but now her mother-in-law invariably referred to her as " that widow ". Josephine had given two large dinner parties in 1799 and at neither of them had any of her relatives by marriage been present. Even Louis, who had at one time been her good friend, had gradually stopped visiting her.

Josephine was a little saddened that she had never liked her husband's family, because she liked most people. But those Corsicans! They were not at all the same as her French friends. She had been perfectly at ease with everyone at Gohier's the night before. They had been her kind and they understood her easy-going Creole ways, but the Bonapartes positively frightened her. When she spoke of them to her intimates, Josephine called them " those monsters ".

In one sense, of course, the family had an advantage over her. Josephine, who liked to be fair, admitted that she had been unwise to cause quite so much scandal in Paris, but she had always believed Napoleon to be so infatuated with her that what the family thought was unimportant. She was still, in fact, confident of this, but now there were undoubtedly some awkward facts to be explained away.

One of the reasons for the family's hostility was that they hated to see her squandering good Bonaparte money. When the General had gone to Egypt he had left Josephine an annual income of forty thousand francs which Joseph had conscientiously administered on her behalf. In addition, her husband had sent her two large remittances while he had been away. This should have been more than enough for her to live on in comfort, and Bonaparte had every reason to expect that her finances would be in good order. Moreover, since very little that had political implications ever escaped him, the General might discover that Fouché had been making her payments from the secret funds. Josephine thought it possible Bonaparte would be annoyed to find that his wife had been employed as a police spy.

In spite of all this income, Josephine was deeply in debt. She was both extravagant and careless, buying whatever took her fancy and putting the bills away without checking them or paying them. As a result, she now owed nearly a million francs to various tradesmen. Nor was this the sum of her indebtedness. Four months after the General had left for Egypt, she had bought a château. Malmaison, with its forty-five acres of parks and woodland, was a beautiful estate on the Seine between Saint-Germain-en-Laye and Paris, but unfortunately it was not paid for. She still owed three hundred thousand francs on it.

The Bonapartes, of course, had disapproved of the purchase of Malmaison. They had said that she had bought it as a child buys a doll, without considering how long she would want it. That was really unfair. The General had wanted a country house, and Joseph, who had complained so loudly when she bought Malmaison, had himself purchased a large estate at Mortefontaine where he played the *grand seigneur* to his heart's content. Although they seemed to begrudge her every franc she spent, the Bonapartes had done well out of Liberty, Equality, and Fraternity since they had fled penniless from Corsica six years ago. Everyone admitted that Malmaison was worth the purchase price, and besides it had been conveniently near Madame Campan's school for girls where Hortense was a boarder.

At first Hortense used to spend an occasional week-end with her mother at Malmaison, but that had stopped before long. One afternoon, quite by chance, when she had been taking Hortense to her weekly class at the Despreaux Dancing School in the Rue de Mont-Blanc, Josephine had met Hippolyte Charles again. She had not seen that young gentleman since he had been cashiered and nearly shot by Bonaparte in Italy,[14] and she had listened with sympathy to the story of his misfortunes. Hippolyte Charles had fallen upon hard times. His talents were not of the type which were of much assistance to him when it came to earning a living. Because she was genuinely distressed by the hardships Charles claimed to have suffered—and all for her sake!—Josephine had gone to her former lover, Barras, and sought his aid. One more bit of patronage made little difference to Barras, and he still retained some affection for Josephine. At all events, through his influence Charles had been established as a purveyor to the army and acquired an interest in the firm of Bodin, which supplied rations and forage to the forces.

Not long afterwards Charles had begun to visit Malmaison. He was really an extremely good-looking young man, and very much Josephine's sort of person, full of witty stories and quite without that seriousness which made some people so dull. Before long Hippolyte Charles had taken up permanent residence at Malmaison.

Charles was not discreet. (How could he have been, when he was now, for the second time, indulging in a hobby which many would have considered the most dangerous in France?) Very soon Hippolyte Charles was acting as though Malmaison belonged to him, ordering the servants about and lording it over the villagers. This had given rise to a good deal of comment, and had completed the estrangement with the Bonaparte family.

Now, as her carriage went spanking along through Burgundy, Josephine turned all these matters over in her mind, and as she did so her anxiety grew . . .

Early on the morning of 16th October, Madame Bourrienne, the wife of Bonaparte's secretary, was on her way to meet her husband in Paris. Soon after passing the first post-house, Madame Bourrienne recognised Louis Bonaparte inside a berlin going in the opposite direction. She waved to him, and Louis ordered his postillion to stop. While they chatted by the road-side, Madame Bourrienne told Louis that his brother would be passing through Sens, where he planned to dine with Bourrienne's mother. When Louis drove on a few minutes later, he was still unaware that the General had suddenly changed his plans and taken the Bourbonnais road. Not long afterwards Madame Bourrienne met another berlin containing Josephine and Hortense, but since both mother and daughter were asleep and the carriages were going fast, she did not attempt to stop the General's wife.[15]

At Châlon-sur-Saône, when Josephine's carriage halted to change horses, she heard that Bonaparte had taken the Bourbonnais road from Lyons. She had missed him. There was now no way in which she could get to him before his brothers. For the first time the full seriousness of her situation came home to her. Three years ago she had married prudently, intending to settle down to a secure future. Now she had put it all in jeopardy. She was impossibly in debt; she did not even own the little house on the Rue de la Victoire; she had two children whom she loved and whose future depended entirely upon their stepfather; she had no place to go, no one to turn to. And she was thirty-seven years old.

Josephine turned back to Paris in black despair.

*   *   *

There is no direct evidence as to what Bonaparte had decided to do about Josephine's infidelities. Bourrienne says that he had not mentioned divorce since the previous February and had apparently put the matter out of his mind.[16] Probably, if Josephine had been on hand to meet him, Bonaparte would have behaved as he had on previous occasions. He would have reproached her; she would have given explanations and excuses; she would have claimed that her enemies slandered her; and she would have wept and been forgiven.

It seems likely, indeed, that Bonaparte had already reconciled himself to this course. For more than three years he had been deeply in love with Josephine, and that love had not yet died. Perhaps he still hoped that it would not, that no matter what had happened during the time of separation, they would be able to re-establish their former relationship and go on as before. He had known that his wife had had lovers before he married her, and it had meant nothing to him. In spite of his imaginative insight in other matters, his conscious views on sex were as pragmatic as his views on war. It was his chief weakness in both spheres. To Bonaparte there was nothing mysterious about sex, certainly nothing sacramental. A few years later, when he was Emperor, he arranged to have an actress who had taken his fancy visit his apartments. She arrived while he was discussing some high official matter, and his Mameluke servant, Rustum, interrupted the conference to announce her arrival. " Tell her to wait," the Emperor said. Half an hour later Rustum appeared again to remind his master that the lady was still waiting. " Tell her to take her clothes off," the Emperor said, and returned to the business that absorbed his attention. When Rustum appeared for the third time, Napoleon looked up impatiently and said: " Tell her to go home."

By then he had grown more callous in such affairs, but the roots of that attitude had always been a part of him. Moreover, his Corsican upbringing inclined him to the view that wives were frail creatures who needed the close supervision of their husbands —an opinion which, whatever its origins, was more than justified in the case of Josephine. He may also have blamed himself for having neglected his marital responsibilities. He had, after all, been away a long time. And there had been his own affair with Madame Fourés in Egypt. Bonaparte may well have told himself that the just and sensible thing to do would be to let bygones be bygones.

However, such a decision could not have been reached without pain and inner conflict, even by a man who attempted to be as completely rational as Bonaparte did. His emotions must have been tense even before his mother opened the door, and the physical strain of his long journey may also have had an effect upon him.

Certainly Josephine's absence on the morning of 16th October came as a disproportionately great shock to Bonaparte. He immediately concluded that Josephine, unable to face him because of her guilt, had fled at the news of his landing. Possibly she and Hippolyte Charles had fled together. He refused to believe the perfectly plausible story that Josephine had set out to meet him and had missed him on the road.

Years later, when he finally did divorce his wife, he had clearly not forgotten the terrible impression of desolation which the empty house had made on his mind, and he referred to it even then with bitterness.[17] On the morning of 16th October, as he went from room to room of the little house where he had formerly been so happy, there was an emptiness in his heart which corresponded to the empty rooms. For the first time in his life he became aware of the terrible fragility of human affection.

Bonaparte stormed and cursed and vowed he would divorce his wife. Poor Eugene, who had come home with him, crept upstairs to his own room and shut himself in. There was no point in talking to the distraught and anguished man who wept and raged and ordered the servants to pack all Josephine's jewels and clothing and deposit them at the door with the concierge.

Letizia also refrained from reasoning with her son. She had foreseen this day, for she had long ago assessed Josephine's character. " That widow " possessed nearly every trait which Letizia held in contempt. Certainly a fickle Creole adventuress had never been good enough to marry a Bonaparte. Probably, too, the pious Letizia had never considered Napoleon and Josephine validly married. They had, after all, only been united by a civil ceremony hurriedly performed by the mayor of the second *arrondissement* of Paris.

The General went to his study and sat moodily before the fire. In the course of the day the rest of the family descended upon the Rue de la Victoire—the good Joseph, indignant that his sound advice to Josephine had been disregarded; the impassioned Lucien, talking of the family honour; Elisa, with her biting tongue, also talking of the family honour but thinking of the family fortune; Pauline, pretty and provocative and pointed, still in love with her husband, General Leclerc, and quite unable to sympathize with a woman with whom she had much in common; Jerome and Caroline, both too young to have any voice in such an important family council, but learning the Bonaparte style. With them too was Joseph's wife, Julie, but she took no part in the acrimonious discussion, perhaps because she was French rather than Corsican and perhaps also because she felt some pity for any woman who had married into the clan.

Of the blood relatives, only Letizia kept silent that afternoon. She agreed with her children, but she was older, wiser, and more resigned. Napoleon's mother was a remarkable woman. In her day she had been a great Corsican beauty, and she was still handsome, with her chestnut hair only lightly flecked with grey, her noble forehead, and her great, luminous eyes. But already on her face there was that shade of pensive sorrow which was to deepen with the years. While her children bombarded Napoleon with their importunities, Letizia remained silent and thought about the end.

Not everyone agreed with the Bonaparte family that a divorce was the correct solution. Both Bourrienne and the banker Collot attempted to dissuade the General, Bourrienne because he had always been treated kindly by Josephine and Collot because he was above all things anxious that a Government capable of decreeing forced loans be thrown out as soon as possible.[18] Collot was afraid that a domestic scandal would damage Bonaparte's public image. Paris was far more inclined to view a wronged husband with amusement than with sympathy.

The General, however, was adamant.

" No! " he said. " She must go! No matter what people say. They will gossip for a day or two and then forget all about it."

It was an interesting day at the Rue de la Victoire, and many of the participants must have enjoyed it thoroughly.

*   *   *

Bonaparte, however, never allowed personal problems to interfere with his larger designs. Josephine might be his wife, but power was his mistress. On his first night in Paris he went to see Gohier, the President of the Directory. In spite of the acclaim with which the Five Hundred had greeted the news of his arrival, the General was somewhat uneasy as to how the Government would receive him.

Gohier was friendly but non-committal. Bonaparte said to him:

" President, the news I received in Egypt was so alarming that I did not hesitate to leave the Army and come to share your perils."

Gohier replied: "They were indeed great, General, but we have gloriously surmounted them. You have arrived in time to join us in celebrating the numerous triumphs of your comrades-in-arms."[19]

This was not precisely the reaction for which Bonaparte had hoped. He left shortly afterwards, having first arranged to present himself to the full Directory the following morning.

The General laid his uniform aside before he set out for the Luxembourg on 18th October. From now on it was part of his policy to wear unostentatious civilian dress, for he knew that such small details would help allay fears that he was planning a military *coup*, and Bonaparte never neglected details. This morning, therefore, he wore a round civilian hat and a plain olive-green coat, although—as a reminder of the romantic Orient and his victories there—a magnificent Turkish scimitar encrusted with precious stones was suspended by his side from a silken sash.

A number of people had been waiting outside No. 6 Rue de la Victoire in the hope of catching a glimpse of their hero, and by the time Bonaparte reached the Luxembourg a large crowd was following him. They commented freely to each other on his appearance, remarking that he was as brown as an Arab and that he now wore his hair short and unpowdered in the latest style. When the guard of the Directory turned out to present arms to the little civilian figure, the crowd cheered.

The General's valet, Constant, has left us a detailed description of the great man at this time:

> On his return from Egypt the Emperor was very thin and sallow, his skin was copper-coloured, his eyes sunken, and his figure, though perfect, also very thin . . . His forehead was very high and bare; his hair thin, especially on the temples, but very fine and soft, and a rich brown colour; his eyes deep and blue, expressing in an almost incredible manner the various emotions by which he was affected, sometimes gentle and caressing, sometimes severe and even inflexible. His mouth was very fine, his lips straight and rather firmly closed, particularly when irritated. His

teeth, without being very regular, were very white and sound, and
he never suffered from them . . . His whole frame was handsomely
proportioned, though at this time his extreme leanness prevented
the beauty of his features being especially noticed and had an
injurious effect on his whole physiognomy.[20]

The five Directors received General Bonaparte politely but
without enthusiasm. To all appearances this interview was no
more than the normal report of a military commander to his
civilian superiors. The Directors listened in silence to the
General's account of the campaign in Egypt. They could do
nothing else, for they lacked the detailed information which would
have been necessary to question him closely. When Bonaparte
spoke of the Mamelukes, the Turks, Aboukir, Cairo, or St Jean
d'Acre, the civilian heads of Government had no means of verify-
ing his facts and figures and no basis on which to advance any
contrary opinion. Nevertheless, the suspicion and hostility in the
room was palpable.

After delivering an inaccurately optimistic report on the French
Army of Egypt, Bonaparte ended dramatically. Placing his hand
on his sword hilt, he declared:

" Citizen Directors, I swear that I will never draw this sword
except in the defence of the Republic and its government."[21]

This noble sentiment being received in silence, Bonaparte went
on to say that he would be willing to be of help to the Directory
" as the head of an army, if you should see fit to confer one upon
me, or even as a simple gunner as I did in the early days of my
military life, which I have never forgotten." Since the five Directors did no more than look at him stolidly, the General added with
a touch of defiance: " I still know how to load and lay a gun, just
as I did at Toulon."[22]

The Directors had already discussed among themselves what
they should do with Bonaparte and had decided that at all costs
he should be got out of France. In spite of some initial opposition
from Barras and Sieyès, they had at last agreed to offer him the
command of any French army he might choose.[23] Because of his

previous successes in Italy and because the situation in that theatre was the most critical, there had been a general feeling that Bonaparte should be employed there. Barras had cynically commented that the General would be unlikely to want to return to Italy since he had already made his fortune out of that country, but the Directory now offered Bonaparte a field command, mentioning the Italian theatre as a possibility.

This, of course, was the last thing the General wanted, and he made haste to retract his offer of military service. Now that he was in the house, he had no intention of being shoved out into the garden again. He thanked the Directors for their confidence in him, but said that he had not meant that he could take up a command immediately. Prolonged campaigning had undermined his health. Later, when he was feeling better, he would gladly serve wherever the Government saw fit to employ him.

These assurances did not make much impression on the Directors, who were professionally accustomed to dissimulation, but Gohier, in his capacity as President, replied for all of them in a pompous little speech which nicely matched the General's. Gohier ended with the classical antithesis so popular with his generation. The Directory, he said, did not wage war in the hope of concluding a satisfactory peace but in the hope of winning fresh victories. " And the Government is too well aware, Citizen General, of your former services and of the republican sentiments which animate you, not to hasten to employ your talents for the complete accomplishment of its liberal projects."[24]

After this there was nothing much to say. The meeting had already gone on for two and a half hours, and even the professional politicians and the man who hoped to supplant them could endure only so much hypocrisy. After a further exchange of coldly formal compliments, the General took his leave.

Bonaparte was well satisfied with his morning's work, for he now knew that he had nothing to fear from the Directors. Quite obviously they did not dare to impeach him for the desertion of his army or for breaking the quarantine. He had retained the initiative.

*   *   *

Late on the night of 18th October, after five days' useless journeying, Josephine and Hortense arrived back in Paris. During the past forty-eight hours Josephine had had time to realize the peril of her position, and by now she was in a state of extreme agitation. Hortense went upstairs to her room and Josephine hurried to the General's study. A light shining from under the study door showed that Bonaparte was in, but the door was locked and Josephine received no response to her knocking.

The events of that night are known to us only in their main outlines and at second hand. A few years later, Madame de Rémusat had an account of the episode from Josephine, and Barras, of all people, claimed that Bonaparte spoke to him about it, complaining to him of his wife's infidelities,[25] but this is as unlikely as much else in Barras' unreliable *Memoirs*. Of those who were in the house on the night of 18th October, only Eugene has left us any account of the quarrel between his mother and step-father, and very naturally Eugene passes quickly over the scene. Certainly Josephine wept and pleaded for a long time in the hall outside the closed study door without getting any answer from her husband. At last in desperation she sent for Eugene and Hortense to come down and add their pleas to hers. Bonaparte was fond of both his step-children, feeling for them with almost the same Corsican intensity as for his own blood relatives. Eugene especially was like a son to him and had always given him good reason for pride.

What the two step-children said we have no sure way of knowing; the speeches Madame Junot attributes to them are almost—but not quite—too banal even for the expression of French emotions in 1799.[26] At all events, there came the sound of a chair being scraped back and of footsteps crossing the study floor.

Then the door slowly opened. Josephine, shaken with sobs and nearly fainting, was now stretched out almost prostrate on the small back staircase nearby. Bonaparte appeared in the doorway, his face haggard with strain. Without a word he went across to his wife, raised her to her feet, and embraced her. They went into the study together and Eugene and Hortense crept quietly up the stairs.[27]

Once he had taken the decision to forgive his wife, Bonaparte held nothing back. There were no reproaches, no stormy scenes, no anger and no petty resentment. He paid all her debts without complaint—although he carefully scrutinised the accounts and was quick to detect any overcharging. He did not even make any move against young Hippolyte Charles, who was allowed to slip back unmolested into his own world of dubious deals and quick profits.

Josephine, for her part, was in future a loyal and faithful wife. There were no more lovers, and although she remained quite incapable of restraining her extravagance or keeping out of debt, Bonaparte had no further cause for serious complaint. Indeed, as time went by, Josephine grew genuinely to love her husband. There was something at once pathetic and ironic about the new relationship between them. Later, when the seven years' difference in their ages had grown as such gaps do, the Empress Josephine would proudly boast to the maid who came in to wake her in the morning: " The Emperor spent the night with me last night." After the divorce Josephine would plead for a short visit from her ex-husband, and although it is difficult to be certain of any sincerity when an individual has as much power as Napoleon had, Josephine had then no need to pretend to an affection she did not feel.

The reconciliation, however, marked an end as well as a new beginning. Between 16th and 18th of October something died in Bonaparte; some final brightness fell from the air. This, however, was not at once apparent, and it was long before Josephine suspected any change. The ardour which formerly had frightened and repelled her was now replaced by a comfortable comradeship more to her liking. Bonaparte, indeed, retained an affection for his wife as long as she lived.

Nevertheless, after the October reconciliation nothing was ever quite the same again between them. With sexual love, as with his happy boyhood and with his Corsican nationalism, the theme of Bonaparte's spiritual isolation was repeated in another key. It was part of his greatness that he was unwilling to compromise with life, to accept success in lieu of victory. But nothing human is indomitable, and he could escape from each defeat only by cutting off a part of himself. He survived by separation, as a wild creature caught in a trap gnaws off its paw in order to go free.

Now, in this climacteric year of 1799 when all the course of his life was set beyond the possibility of deviation, he found that although he could forgive he could not go back. He was never again to feel real love for Josephine, or for any other woman.

Being Bonaparte, he understood this and fought against it. From now on he filled his life with love affairs, with actresses, singers, ladies-in-waiting. Often, for a short time, he thought that he had found the lost thing, but he never had.

*   *   *

On the morning of 19th October, when Lucien Bonaparte called on his brother, he was shown upstairs to the bedroom. He found Napoleon and Josephine in bed together. Lucien's handsome, Italianate face darkened at this domestic vignette, for he had no doubt that his reception here was due to Josephine's desire to flaunt her triumph, but he had the good sense not to expostulate with Napoleon. So did the rest of the family. This did not prevent them, however, from saying the most bitter things about Josephine to all their acquaintances.

Two days later Lucien visited his brother again, this time to discuss the political situation. For some time Lucien had been working closely with the group of men around Sieyès and he was therefore able to tell the General much of the ex-abbé's plans.

Beneath all the shifting alliances and intrigue in Paris, four main political forces could be discerned: the moderates grouped around Sieyès, the Decadents who wished to maintain the *status quo,* the Jacobins, and the royalists. The moderates had so far been completely ineffectual, and the supporters of the present Government had been able to retain power because the pressures exerted by their opponents had cancelled each other out.

Barras openly referred to this policy as that of the " see-saw ": the nation was told that with any shift to the Left the Jacobins would bring back the Terror and that with any shift to the Right the royalists would bring back the avenging Bourbons. Both Jacobins and royalists displayed an amazing lack of political sense. Much as the Directory was despised, the people of France wanted no change which would result in Jourdan's " resurrection of the pikes ". And the exiled Bourbons, now as later, had learned nothing and forgotten nothing. They tactlessly kept reminding the French that when the monarchy was restored the people as well as the government would have to pay for having killed the king and queen. The emigré nobles boasted that they would regain all their privileges, so that army officers feared for the loss of their commissions and the peasants for the loss of their land. Madame de Staël was patently right when she said: " The noblemen of France consider themselves to be the compatriots of the noblemen of every nation rather than the fellow-citizens of Frenchmen." Because the Jacobins and royalists were both so stupidly intransigent, even the Government of the Directory appeared preferable to either of them.

The Parisian proletariat and lower middle-class, which so short a time before had astonished Europe by its energy, was now sunk in apathy. By 1799 the men of the faubourgs wanted only to be left in peace and to earn a reasonable living. The peasants wanted to keep their land and their freedom from feudal oppression, but they hated Jourdan's conscription law which mustered their sons into the army.

In the Council of Five Hundred rather more than half of the deputies were of the Left, and about sixty of these were Jacobins. One hundred and forty deputies supported the moderate policies of Sieyès, and the remainder were royalists of the extreme Right.

The Council of Ancients had belonged for the most part to the ignoble Plain of the old Convention of '93. These men had tolerated the Terror so long as they could themselves survive, and the passage of time had not improved their characters. Three-quarters of them were conservative, bourgeois, and anxious to call a halt to the Revolution. They habitually spoke of the Jacobins as the " liberticide faction ", and they could be counted upon to support any dictator who promised to protect their lives and their property and to keep the social order by and large as it then was.[28]

In the Directory itself only Gohier and Moulin believed that the present system of Government could survive. Gohier, however, could be counted on to cling to power to the end, for he loved it and identified himself in his own mind with the Republic. Moulin was too stupid and colourless to count.[29] He almost always voted with Gohier in the Directory. Neither of these men could be bribed, not so much because they were honest as because they had already attained the highest office in the state and could be offered nothing more attractive.

Barras was utterly discredited and had little following, but he still controlled the police through the minister Fouché. More than anyone else, Barras was responsible for the corruption of the Government. He knew that a change had to come, and his only concern was to profit by it, whatever it was. This meant that Barras could always be bought, if the price was right.

Most of this General Bonaparte had known or guessed already, but Lucien then went on to tell him about the conspiracy which centred on the ex-abbé Sieyès. Perhaps " conspiracy " was almost too strong a word for the rather vague plot which had been developed at a meeting on 28th September, when Lucien, Sieyès and some others had met to formulate their plans. According to

Lucien, the ex-abbé hoped to stage a *coup d'état* which would replace the five Directors with an executive of three Consuls who would serve for ten years; a senate nominated for life would replace the Council of Ancients; and a Legislative Council would be elected by a system of graduated universal suffrage. Sieyès would also abolish the forced loans and repeal the Law of Hostages, by which the relatives of royalist emigrés were being penalized for the political sympathies of their kinsmen. Apostacy had not killed Sieyès' taste for metaphysics and he talked a good deal about the reasons for his system and the beneficial results to be expected from it.

General Bonaparte listened to all this with interest and at the end told Lucien that he agreed with Sieyès on all points. The General added that he was prepared to act as a shield to the wise men of the Republic against the revolt of the faubourgs, just as he had served on 13th Vendémiaire as a shield for the Convention against the revolt of the royalist sections.

Lucien told his brother he was certain that France would give its overwhelming support to Sieyès' programme if it went to a referendum and that a majority could be counted upon in the Council of Ancients. However, he foresaw difficulties in obtaining ratification in the Council of Five Hundred.

The General did not commit himself, but at the end of Lucien's exposition turned to the deputy Roederer, who in constitutional matters was Sieyès' disciple, and asked: " Do you believe the thing is possible?"

" It is three-quarters done," was Roederer's reply.

Bonaparte, however, was in no hurry to ally himself with anyone. He saw clearly that what France needed was an end to party strife, a " nationalization " of the Revolution. He was determined that when he came to power he would not be the representative or the captive of any faction, and he planned a state in which men of all shades of political opinion could work together for the national good. At the moment Bonaparte, with his military glory, his popularity with the people, and his non-political reputation, did stand above the factions, and he encouraged each of them to hope that he would help their particular cause. Jacobins, moderates and royalists all came to visit the General at No. 6 Rue de la Victoire and all were treated the same. Bonaparte was friendly, gracious, interested in all they had to say, but he did not reveal his own intentions.

Although his home was always open to the society of Paris, the General went out very rarely. When he did leave the house, he made himself as inconspicuous as possible, and a special grating was fixed to the front of his box in the theatre so that the audience could not stare at him. But in spite of this modest behaviour, the papers of the Left were already beginning to print hard things about his desertion of the Army of Egypt and to predict that if Bonaparte saved France the price of salvation might be high.

In 1803, speaking to Madame de Rémusat, Bonaparte recalled his tactics at this time:

> I was very careful. It was one of the periods of my life when I acted with the soundest judgment. I saw the Abbé Sieyès and promised him that his wordy Constitution would be put into effect. I received the leading Jacobins and Bourbon agents. I listened to advice from everyone, but gave advice only in the interests of my own plans. I hid myself from the people, because I knew that when the moment came, curiosity to see me would bring them running after me. Everyone was caught in my nets and when I became head of the state there was not a party in France that did not build some special hope on my success.[30]

In the middle of October, however, the General still hoped to obtain power by constitutional methods and therefore had no intention of joining the plot of Sieyès, Lucien and their followers. Bonaparte believed there was a good chance he might become a member of the Directory and was confident that once inside the Government he could dominate it. If, on the contrary, he staged a *coup d'état*, his regime would be marked with the stigma of illegality and violence. Many would see him as merely another ambitious soldier, and those who would otherwise have served him willingly would have to be coerced. The General had no scruples about coercion, but many practical objections to it. He said that there were only two powers in the world, the power of the sword and the power of the spirit, and that the power of the spirit was always the stronger.

In any case, he felt a personal repugnance to Sieyès. That dry and timid apostate, who personified the frivolous theorizing of the Revolution, was all that the General most despised. Moreover, Bonaparte had no wish to ally himself to a politician who was a regicide hateful to all shades of royalist opinion and who as an ex-abbé was held in contempt by the Catholics, still the overwhelming majority of the nation.

On the night of the 30th Vendémiaire the General, Josephine, and several members of the Institute went to dine with Gohier at the Luxembourg. When Josephine saw that her husband had been seated next to Sieyès at the table, she turned to Gohier and whispered: " What have you done! Sieyès is the man whom Bonaparte most detests! He is his *bête noire.*"[31]

Throughout the meal the two men sat side by side in silence, and Bonaparte did not so much as look at Sieyès. Later in the evening Bonaparte was introduced to General Moreau for the first time. For a long moment the two soldiers regarded each other steadily without speaking, but because Moreau's military reputation had recently been dimmed by his defeat in Italy, it was easy for Bonaparte to be gracious. He smiled warmly and spoke first, saying that he had long looked forward to making Moreau's acquaintance.

Moreau replied: " Yes, but you have come back from Egypt victorious, and I have just returned from Italy after a great defeat."

They discussed war for a while, and Moreau, having reminded his hearers how the Russian and Austrian forces in Italy had outnumbered the French, remarked that the larger army always defeated the smaller. Bonaparte agreed with him, and when Gohier objected—rather tactlessly—that in the Italian campaign of 1796 Bonaparte had in fact defeated greatly superior Austrian forces, the General replied that even then it had always been the larger number which had beaten the smaller.[32]

For Sieyès the evening had been a humiliating experience. Before he took his leave he said to Gohier: " Did you notice the conduct of that insolent little fellow towards a member of a Government who could have had him shot?"[33]

The next afternoon Bonaparte, in company with Monge and Berthollet, visited the Institute. Here, as everywhere these days, the General adopted an unassuming air, discussing the scientific discoveries of the Egyptian expedition with charming modesty. That same day, which according to the revolutionary calendar was the 1st Brumaire,* Lucien Bonaparte, as a compliment to his brother, was elected President of the Council of Five Hundred.

In the evening the General again went to the Luxembourg to see Gohier privately. The pretext of this call was to thank the Director for the previous night's dinner, but Bonaparte soon revealed what he had in mind. Sieyès, he said, was hardly a suitable person to be a Director of the Republic. A number of good citizens had told him how much they regretted Sieyès' having been given high office. Would it not perhaps be a good idea if he were forced to resign? As for the vacancy which would be created in the Directory . . . Well, several people had been kind enough to suggest that General Bonaparte could be of more service to his country as a Director than as a soldier.

Gohier did not like Sieyès, with his insulting patience, his perpetual air of a schoolmaster speaking to a backward class, and his incoherent profundity. Perhaps it was even true that he was a threat to the Republic. But Sieyès was fifty-two years old, a man of some maturity, while Bonaparte was only thirty.

Gohier replied that unfortunately an article of the Constitution explicitly forbade anyone under forty becoming a Director. This was a great pity because otherwise Bonaparte would certainly be

---

* 23rd October.

elected by acclamation. Gohier advised the young man to wait. The day would undoubtedly come when he would be head of the Government. But not, he implied, for another ten years.

Bonaparte had never had much respect for the law as such. As a native of Corsica, where social standards were still those of the Italian Renaissance, he had been brought up to regard the law as an instrument of foreign tyranny and as a soldier on active service he had been accustomed to ignoring legal niceties. Now he argued that in interpreting the Constitution so strictly Gohier was holding to the letter which killed rather than to the spirit which gave life. The General protested that it was by no means personal ambition which induced him to make his proposal, but only a sense of duty to the Republic.

Gohier replied that he sympathized with these views, but that in his eyes nothing could excuse a breach of the Constitution.[34]

When Bonaparte later approached Moulin with the same proposal, he received the same answer—and very naturally so, because Moulin had talked it over with Gohier first and been told what to say.

This refusal caused Bonaparte to reconsider his plans. If he could not seize power legally, he would have to seize it by force, and for the first time he began to prepare for a *coup d'état*. He still did not commit himself to any faction, but rather formed his own by gathering together what Fouché called " a sort of privy council " of his supporters.[35] His brothers Lucien and Joseph; his chief of staff Berthier; the witty and cynical Réal, who had been the public prosecutor for the revolutionary criminal tribunal; Bruix, the Minister of Marine; and Talleyrand became the principals in a new conspiracy which aimed not at implementing Sieyès' constitution, but at putting the General in power.

Fouché was not admitted into the inner circle of the conspirators, although he was well aware that a plot was being formed and more than once broadly hinted that he was prepared to help.[36] The General needed Fouché's assistance, for the Minister of Police could be a serious obstacle to any *coup*, but Bonaparte did not want to associate too openly with a man of Fouché's reputation. Besides, the conspirators did not need to take him into their confidence. If the *coup* succeeded, Fouché would help in any case; if it failed he could be trusted to betray them.

At this time Bonaparte seriously considered an alliance with the Jacobins. General Jourdan had offered him the leadership of the party, and the men of the *Manège* had much to recommend them to the General. The Jacobins were a disciplined party, full of energy, and with experience of governing. Although they were deeply hated throughout France, they were still popular with the Parisian proletariat and influential with the army, who believed that a Jacobin government would be the best guarantee against the return of the emigrés.

On the other hand, if Bonaparte came to power with Jacobin support, his regime could never be popular. Worse still, since the Jacobins would not accept some of the measures he considered necessary, he would have to face a revolt of his supporters soon after he took office. Bonaparte, however, did not refuse Jourdan's offer. He was very courteous to his fellow general, flattered him, and contrived to give the impression that, while he had not definitely decided to become a Jacobin, this step was probably only a matter of time.

*   *   *

Bonaparte's tenderness for constitutional methods did not prevent him from giving tasks to the generals who had accompanied him from Egypt. His young men received their orders with enthusiasm.

Murat had already been getting bored in Paris where there was little for him to do except court Caroline. This was presenting some difficulties, both because Bonaparte was cool to the idea and because Caroline herself, who was by no means cool, was a boarder in Madame Campan's school for girls at Saint-Germain. Madame Campan, who had been a lady-in-waiting to Queen

Marie Antoinette, had very strict ideas about what was proper for her charges, and Murat found it hard to conduct a really satisfactory courtship under these circumstances. Still the days passed pleasantly enough for him. He had ordered a batch of new uniforms, some of which he had designed himself; and he had met many of his old friends and made them envious of his exploits in Egypt. But he was anxious for his General to get down to business. Murat could not understand the reason for all the delay. It would be such a simple matter to throw the lawyers out and begin running the country as though it were an army.

Bonaparte told Murat that he was to win over the three cavalry regiments stationed in the capital, the 9th and 21st Dragoons and the 21st Chausseurs. The job should not be too difficult, since two of these regiments had served under Bonaparte in Italy and remembered him affectionately as the " little corporal ". Another favourable circumstance was that the commanding officer of the 9th Dragoons was Colonel Sebastiani, a Corsican and a friend of the Bonapartes. Murat went about his work with gusto.

Marmont had also been finding his return to France disappointing. A coolness had developed between him and his wife —he suspected that she had taken a lover during his absence— and so Marmont too was glad to have something to do. The General ordered him to make sure that the artillery would not oppose any move to overthrow the Government, a particularly important task this, for if it came to street-fighting a few well-placed guns could cause a great deal of trouble. Bonaparte gave Marmont much more explicit instructions than he had given Murat. Marmont was to report on all artillery officers in Paris, on where the gun parks were, where the artillery horses were stabled, where the gunners' barracks were located, and where the battery commanders lived.[37]

Little Berthier was taken into the heart of the conspiracy, which was more than Bonaparte did for any of his other soldiers. Berthier spent much of his time at No. 6 Rue de la Victoire, and

on the days when he was not listening to the civilians talk conspiracy, he was over at the Ministry of War discussing politics
with the officers of the General Staff. Berthier was completely
happy, for he was reunited with Madame Visconti.

Lannes, who was in the process of divorcing his wife, was also
glad to be employed again. Bonaparte assigned him the task of
seducing the loyalty of the infantry. This was an ideal job for
Lannes because when there were no fortresses to storm or battles
to fight he liked nothing better than to talk to good soldiers of his
own arm of the service. Lannes never forgot that he had once
been a grenadier, and although he never allowed his grenadiers
to forget it either, the infantry swore by him.

There was, however, one soldier in Paris who gave Bonaparte
some cause for anxiety. Bernadotte, who had been eased out of his
post as Minister of War in August, had not yet come to the Rue
de la Victoire to pay his compliments. This was the more remarkable because Bernadotte had been one of Bonaparte's divisional
commanders in Italy in '96.

The General thought he knew the reason for Bernadotte's coolness. A number of years ago, when he had still been a struggling
gunner officer with no prospects, Bonaparte had been engaged
to a sweet young girl from Marseilles called Désirée Clary. His
elder brother Joseph had married Désirée's sister, Julie, and had
been presented with a generous dowry by Julie's father, who was
a wealthy merchant. Young Napoleon, attracted by the idea of
marriage and feeling that a good dowry would help his career,
had courted Désirée. At first M. Clary had disapproved of his
daughter marrying a penniless artillery officer. " No! " he had
declared when the suggestion was put to him. " One Bonaparte in
the family is enough! " But Napoleon had gradually worn down
the father's resistance and gained the daughter's affection. Then
he had come to Paris and met Josephine. Madame Beauharnais'
sophisticated manners, her air of being a great lady, her knowledge of the world, and her complaisance had been in sharp contrast to Désirée's healthy provincialism.[38] When Josephine became

Napoleon's mistress, he forgot all about the little girl from Marseilles whom he had intended to marry.

Désirée had been saddened by this treatment. She wrote a pathetic letter to Napoleon, suggesting that she would continue to love him through all the long years of spinsterhood which lay ahead and assuring him that she wished him every success. Shortly afterwards she had married Bernadotte.

Bernadotte was a big, hawk-nosed Gascon whose close-set black eyes were always sharply looking to the main chance. It was whispered that there was Moorish blood in his veins, and it was also said—on better evidence—that he was intriguing with the royalists as well as with the Jacobins. Although he was undeniably shrewd, Bernadotte was not a particularly good general, being too cautious to seize fleeting opportunities and too vain to work well with any colleague. The time was to come when Napoleon would make him a Marshal of the Empire, but this was because the Emperor retained an affection for Désirée, and something of a guilty conscience, rather than because he had any illusions about Bernadotte's military ability.

The suggestion had been made that the two Councils hold an official banquet to honour General Bonaparte and General Moreau, but since some Jacobin members of the Five Hundred objected to this, it had been decided to pay for the banquet by private subscription. On 26th October two deputies approached Bernadotte with the request that he subscribe to the banquet.

Bernadotte replied: " I believe that the dinner should be postponed until Bonaparte has satisfactorily explained why he abandoned his army in Egypt. Moreover, a man who has violated the quarantine laws could easily be carrying the plague, and I don't care to dine with *un pestiféré*."[39]

Quite possibly Bernadotte meant exactly what he said. He was never one to take avoidable risks.

This attitude of Bernadotte's was reported to Bonaparte, but when someone told him that the former Minister of War had recommended to the Directory that he be arrested and shot for deserting the Army of Egypt, Bonaparte refused to believe it. Talking it over with Bourrienne, the General said that Bernadotte was a stubborn man who would stick to his republican principles, but that fortunately he was not ambitious. He added: " If he should become ambitious, he would dare anything."[40]

Napoleon was seldom so completely wrong in his assessment of a man's character. Bernadotte had always been consumed with ambition and jealousy, but he would never run any great risk to achieve his ends.

*   *   *

On 27th October Bonaparte made another of his rare public appearances, when he went for the second time to the Institute to read a paper on the scientific discoveries of the Egyptian expedition. The learned men of France were greatly impressed as they listened to the General speaking of the Rosetta Stone, the ancient monuments of the Pharaohs, and the possibility of a Suez Canal. Behind Bonaparte's thought there was a force almost more remarkable than the penetration and accuracy of the thought itself. The General was aware of this particular quality in himself and later summed it up in one of his striking phrases—" Energy is the well-spring of intelligence."

That same night Bonaparte heard how Barras had told the Directors it would be useless to offer him the Italian command because he had already made his fortune in that country. The General was furious, for this sort of talk could well be dangerous.

In the first place, it was indubitably true. Immediately before Bonaparte had left to take up the command of the Army of Italy in 1796 he had been so poor that Josephine's lawyer had urged her not to marry him. Only a few months previously he had roamed the streets of Paris as a half-pay artillery officer, hungry, cold, and without a sou in his pockets. At times he had been forced to live on his aide-de-camp's gambling winnings.[41] He had had a brief period of fame at Toulon and had won some notoriety for having fired the whiff of grapeshot on the 13th Vendémiaire, but there had been dozens of other officers of equal or greater reputation. He had come back from Italy as more than a conqueror, famous, powerful, and if not wealthy, certainly comfortably well off. On the other hand, he had replenished the Government's coffers with millions of francs' worth of loot and had saved the Directory from a disastrous financial crisis. More than once, the spoils of the Italian campaign had been all that stood between the Republic and bankruptcy.

If at the same time Bonaparte had improved his own and his family's fortunes, was there anyone so mean as to begrudge it to him or to use it now as propaganda against him? There was. Nothing was too mean for Barras. And in a Paris where revolutionary ardour had faded and where most citizens went to bed hungry every night, any suggestion that the longed-for saviour of the nation had made a personal profit from his victories might be enough to damage his legend irretrievably.

The General knew that he had little with which to reproach himself in this matter. Money was unimportant to him for its own sake: his ambition soared much higher than any vulgar desire to enrich himself. Nevertheless the accusation of Barras was to this extent true: that Italy, if it had not made Bonaparte rich, had at least provided him with the necessary competence to make him independent.

He saw the full extent of the danger as soon as he heard the report. The next day, 28th October, he attended a formal sitting of the Directory for the second time and gave Barras the lie to his face. Any money he had made in Italy, he said, had been from the silver mines of Hydria, a purely private venture. He looked Barras straight in the eye and added: " If I made a fortune in Italy, it was not at the expense of the Republic." When Barras failed to reply, the General went on to say that if he had been venal, he could have enriched himself a thousand times over. He was not now a rich man. He had come back from Egypt poorer than when he left.[42]

None of the five Directors around the table could meet his gaze, for all of them had profited from their office far more than the General had ever done, and Sieyès and Barras in particular were rotten with the love of money. The Directors assured Bonaparte in the most fulsome way that no one had meant to impugn his honour; the report he had heard was obviously a malicious misrepresentation. The General left the Luxembourg, satisfied that one danger at least had been overcome.

He was also secure in the knowledge that the banker Collot, who had been an army contractor during the Italian campaign, had advanced him two million francs to finance his bid for power. That money would be repaid from the public purse when the General was head of the state.

The chance sneer of Barras to his fellow Directors was to have grave consequences. Several of those involved in the conspiracy, and particularly Josephine, Réal and Fouché, had for some time been urging Bonaparte to make terms with Barras. There was a certain logic in their position. If the Government was to be betrayed from within—and this to Bonaparte appeared essential —he had to come to terms either with Barras, Sieyès, or Gohier. Gohier had already been approached and had rejected his overtures. Sieyès was as dry and slippery as a snake. Bonaparte had been annoyed to learn that Barras was going about telling everyone that he was " the author of the General's fortunes ", but this by itself would have made no difference. Of much more importance was the fact that Barras could easily be intimidated after the *coup*. Until now the General had rather favoured the idea of an alliance with Barras.

Still, the General had by no means made up his mind. Perhaps the man had been right who had told him a few days ago: " Seek support among the party which calls the friends of the Republic Jacobins, and be assured that Sieyès is at the head of that party."[43] Bonaparte was new to politics and therefore over cautious. At about this time he told Roederer: " No man is more hesitant than I am when I draw up a plan for a military operation.

I exaggerate every danger and every possible obstacle. I fall into a deplorable state of agitation. But that doesn't prevent me from appearing perfectly calm in the presence of those about me. I'm like a woman in childbirth. Then, when I've made my decision, everything is forgotten except what is necessary to implement the decision successfully."

On the 31st October Bernadotte at last paid a courtesy call on his former commander-in-chief. Perhaps Bernadotte believed that since no one in France had so far caught the plague such a visit was now safe. Perhaps, on the other hand, the suspense was finally too much for him.

Bourrienne, who was slaving away at the General's correspondence, heard the story of Bernadotte's first visit only minutes after it was over. Later in the evening he verified the version the General had given him by talking to Josephine, who had also been present. Bernadotte and the General had not got on well together. Bernadotte had the impudence to upbraid Bonaparte for having deserted the Army of Egypt and to say that he regarded that army as lost. (In this, of course, he was absolutely right. The following year, after General Kléber had been assassinated by a Moslem fanatic, the pitiful remnants of that trapped and demoralized army were to surrender to a British expeditionary force.) Worse even than this plain speaking was what Bernadotte had to say about the brilliant and victorious situation of France, the defeat of the Russians, and the French occupation of Genoa.

" I do not despair of the safety of the Republic," Bernadotte had said. " I am certain she can restrain her enemies both abroad —and at home."⁴⁴

At this point Josephine, seeing her husband's rage, had intervened and turned the conversation.

The next day Bonaparte dined with Barras. Fouché and Réal, who had arranged this meeting, waited at the General's house to hear how it turned out. Both the former terrorists, who had been involved in secret police work and had found Barras a sympathetic superior, hoped that he could continue in any reconstituted government. Talleyrand and Roederer were also at the Rue de la Victoire, hoping that the talks with Barras would break down so that Bonaparte and Sieyès would come to terms. It was still early in the evening when the four men heard a carriage approaching. A moment or so later the General came in, frowning and obviously angry. As soon as he entered the room he rounded on Fouché and Réal.

" Well," Bonaparte said, " do you know what this Barras of yours requires? He freely owns that it is impossible to proceed in the present state of things. He is very desirous of having a President of the Republic. But it is himself whom he proposes. What ridiculous pretensions! And this hypocritical wish of his he masks by proposing to invest with the supreme magistracy—whom do you suppose?—Hedouville, that blockhead! Isn't this enough to prove that he wants to fix public attention on himself? What madness! It is impossible to have anything to do with such a man." [45]

Fouché and Réal obtained the General's permission to talk to Barras that same night in a final attempt to make him see reason. They left immediately, and what they had to say to the Director frightened him. Fouché pointed out that Bonaparte was certain to take over the Government. He could do this with Barras or without him, but nothing could prevent the success of the *coup*. It would be advisable to come to terms with the General while there still was time. Barras, impressed by these implied threats, promised to visit Bonaparte early the next day and place himself at his disposal. [46]

However, while Fouché and Réal were frightening Barras, Talleyrand and Roederer had urged another course on the General. Calling for his carriage again, Bonaparte drove to Sieyès' suite at the Luxembourg and reached an understanding with his *bête noire*. Details were not discussed at this first meeting, and the General contented himself with offering his sword. Without actually saying so, Bonaparte contrived to give Sieyès the impression that he was not interested in politics and would perhaps be satisfied to be rewarded with a military command.

Sieyès was not entirely convinced of Bonaparte's disinterestedness. But who else was he to turn to? The *coup* could not hope to succeed unless it had the support of the army, and the ex-abbé was shrewd enough to understand for himself the truth that Fouché was even then trying to impress upon Barras—Bonaparte would overthrow the government in any case. Nevertheless, a few days later when Sieyès was dining with Joseph Bonaparte and M. Cabanis, a member of the Five Hundred and one of the conspirators, he showed himself to be tormented by doubts.

Gloomily Sieyès said: "I am willing to go along with Bonaparte because he is the most civilian of all the generals. But I know what will happen. After we succeed, the General will leave his two colleagues behind—like this—" And as he said the words Sieyès pushed himself between Joseph and Cabanis and stepped in front of them.

When Joseph related this incident to his brother, the General laughed heartily.[47]

Now that things were at last beginning to move, Bernadotte suddenly found himself attracted to Bonaparte's company. A day or two after his first visit he called again at the Rue de la Victoire. The General received him with perfect amicability, but the two men were soon quarrelling.

Bonaparte spoke in sharply critical terms of the agitation prevailing among the extreme Left-wing republicans and said some hard things about the *Manège* Club. Bernadotte took this in bad part, denied that he had been a supporter of the *Manège*, and implied that the violence advocated there had been stirred up by the General's brothers.

Bonaparte burst out angrily, "Well, I tell you plainly I would rather live wild in the woods than in a state of society which affords no security."

"Good God, General, what security would you have?" Bernadotte demanded.

Once again Josephine interrupted just in time to prevent an explosion, and Bernadotte left soon afterwards.[48]

By now General Moreau had been approached and had agreed to help with the *coup*. Bonaparte had presented him with the magnificent Turkish scimitar he had been given by the pasha, Mourad Bey, and Moreau had fallen completely under the younger man's spell. Although some strange scruple prevented Moreau from listening to Bonaparte's plans, he made no other conditions. He said: " I don't want to be let into the secret, but, like the others, I am tired of the yoke of the lawyers. I put myself and my aides-de-camp at your service."

Bonaparte could hardly have wished for more satisfactory support.

*   *   *

On 1st November Bonaparte and Sieyès met at Lucien's house to discuss the plan of the *coup d'état*. This conference lasted only an hour and once again nothing was said about the composition of the new Government. As a rule, Bonaparte and Sieyès found it safer not to meet face to face. Only the urgent desire to see his beloved constitution adopted could have persuaded the ex-abbé to do anything as dangerous as take part in a real conspiracy. As it was, he was often very much afraid. The General, for his part, did nothing to discourage Sieyès' caution, probably feeling that even his charm might wear thin if he saw much of the man he so disliked.

Bonaparte, however, could not escape entirely. Sieyès felt it necessary for his new colleague to be indoctrinated with the right political principles, and sent his friend Roederer to instruct him. Roederer often came at night to the Rue de la Victoire and discoursed at length to Bonaparte on Sieyès' constitutional ideas. The General would listen to all this politely, then Roederer, usually with Talleyrand accompanying him, would report back to the Luxembourg. Talleyrand had to go up first to make sure that

Sieyès had no inquisitive guests, then Roederer would follow him. To dispel suspicion Sieyès always left his door open during these conversations.[49]

During all this time Lucien Bonaparte had been enjoying himself hugely. Almost every night he presided over a meeting of conspirators at Madame Récamier's house at Bagatelle—Lucien at this stage was in love with the beautiful Madame Récamier and preferred to conspire under her admiring eye[50]—but although there was endless talk, nothing very concrete was accomplished. These meetings served to rally some extra support in the Council of Ancients and the Five Hundred, but too many people attended them. In addition to Lucien and Boulay de la Meurthe (who was now an ardent supporter of the General), Fouché lists twenty deputies who could always be found at Madame Récamier's. Groups of conspirators were also meeting almost daily at No. 6 Rue de la Victoire, at Sieyès', at Murat's, at Lannes', and at Berthier's.[51]

Not surprisingly, therefore, the secret was not kept. When Dubois de Crancé, the Minister of War, learned what was going on, he went to Gohier and Moulin with his story, offering to have Bonaparte arrested that same day and promising to supervise the arrest personally. The two directors, however, were incredulous and refused to take any action without positive proof. They even refused to speak to Barras on the subject.

Dubois de Crancé was not put off so easily. Since Gohier and Moulin demanded proof, he provided them with proof. He sent a police agent, who had first-hand knowledge of a great deal of the plot, to the Luxembourg to tell the two Directors what he had heard with his own ears. Gohier and Moulin did not think much of this for they knew that many innocent men had been guillotined on the evidence of just such police spies. And General Bonaparte was not a man to be arrested lightly. Still, since the agent's tale was exceedingly circumstantial, Gohier and Moulin decided to check on it independently. As a precaution, they had the police agent arrested and locked up in a room in the Luxembourg.

The spy at once became frightened. With Paris so full of intrigue, it was not safe to trust anyone. He escaped through a window and reported to Fouché. The Minister of Police convinced Gohier and Moulin that the spy's word was not to be relied upon and then informed Bonaparte of the entire affair.[52]

Time, however, was running out. Unless action was taken soon all hope of overthrowing the Government under a cloak of legality would be lost. An even worse eventuality was possible. The Jacobins had not long been deceived by the General's flattery of Jourdan, and to the men of the *Manége* any political change except one which brought their own party to power was likely to be personally dangerous. The Terror was remembered throughout France, and the Jacobins were fearful of retribution. By the beginning of November there was a real danger that a Jacobin rising might forestall Bonaparte's *coup*.

Fouché watched all this carefully, weighing the strengths and weaknesses of the various factions and wondering whom he should betray. One day he cornered Bourrienne and said to him urgently: "Tell your General to be speedy. If he delays, he is lost."[53]

Fouché was not the only one who grew nervous as the time for the *coup* approached. One night General Bonaparte and Talleyrand sat up late in Talleyrand's home at No. 24 Rue Taitbout, discussing their plans by candlelight. Their conversation had been animated and the city had grown still about them while they talked. Suddenly at one o'clock in the morning there was a loud noise in the street below. They heard the rumble of carriage wheels on the pavé and the clop-clop of the hooves of a cavalry escort. The carriages and horsemen stopped directly in front of Talleyrand's door.

Both men broke off their conversation and looked up. Talleyrand noticed that the General had gone suddenly pale and he records that he had no doubt he did too. The same thought occurred to both simultaneously. Their plans had been betrayed and they were to be arrested.

Without a word Talleyrand stood up and blew out the candles. Then on tiptoe he crept across the hall to a balcony which looked out on the Rue Taitbout. Peering down, he saw what had happened.

On the street was a broken-down carriage, surrounded by an escort of mounted gendarmes. Since the streets of Paris were far from safe in 1799, the gambling rooms of the Palais Royal hired a guard each night at closing time to escort their funds from the gaming house to a bank in the Rue de Clichy. The carriage containing the money had happened to break down tonight exactly in front of Talleyrand's house.[54]

*　　*　　*

On 6th November the official banquet in honour of Bonaparte and Moreau was held in the Temple de la Victoire, the former Church of Saint Sulpice. Bernadotte, Jourdan, and Augereau refused to attend, but the square in front of the church and the adjacent streets were thronged with people waiting to catch a glimpse of their hero. A great crowd of women in the Rue de la Verneuil and the Rue de Boc cried out " *Vive Bonaparte!* " when the General descended from his carriage. Bonaparte was accompanied by Murat, Lannes, Marmont and Berthier, all of whom were already symbols of French military glory, but some of the crowd also shouted " *La paix! La paix!* "

The interior of the Church of Saint Sulpice was smoky, humid and noisy; a military band played popular airs; flags were draped everywhere; and a huge placard proclaimed: " *Soyez unis, vous serez vainqueurs.* " Six hundred guests had paid to be present, and Gohier presided at the head table. A royalist agent, reporting on the banquet to London a fortnight later, mentioned that there were some hisses mingled with the applause when Bonaparte entered the hall, but he may merely have been writing what he thought would please his masters.

In any case, the banquet was not a success. An air of constraint hung over the whole gathering, and this was not alleviated when Bonaparte's aide-de-camp, Duroc, ostentatiously brought his General a small loaf of bread and a half bottle of wine for his meal. Bonaparte refused to touch the dinner prepared for him, and the other guests were unpleasantly reminded that General Hoche had recently died under circumstances which had suggested the possibility of poisoning. The conspirators and their intended victims sat side by side in an atmosphere of mutual suspicion. The absence of the three Jacobin generals was commented upon, and a rumour went around from table to table that they were in the Faubourg St Antoine, plotting a revolt of the sections at the house of Santerre the Brewer, the notorious " king of the faubourgs " who had ordered the roll of drums which had drowned out the last words of Louis XVI on the scaffold.

One of the deputies leaned towards his neighbour and whispered:

" This reminds me of nothing so much as of those funeral feasts the ancient Romans used to give. What are we burying— military glory or liberty?"[55]

The usual toasts were proposed and drunk. Lemercier, the President of the Council of Ancients, raised his glass to " The French Republic! " Lucien drank to the success of French arms on land and sea; Gohier to peace; Moreau to all the faithful allies of the Republic. And General Bonaparte stood up and proposed a toast to " The union of all Frenchmen ".

Shortly afterwards the General slipped quietly out of his place, said good-bye to a few people at the head table, and left the hall, followed a pace behind by Berthier. He had been at the banquet only an hour.

He went directly to Lucien's house in the Rue Verte for a second meeting with Sieyès. The *coup* had been tentatively scheduled for the following day, 17th Brumaire,* and this was supposed to have been the final co-ordinating conference. Sieyès

---

* 8th November.

informed Bonaparte that everything was almost ready but suggested a postponement because Cambacérès, the Minister of Justice, and Lebrun, a deputy, were still wavering. In a day they could probably be talked around. Bonaparte agreed.

Later some remembered that 17th Brumaire had been a Friday and suggested that Bonaparte was too much a Corsican to begin any great venture on a Friday, but this was almost certainly nonsense. The General had too much faith in his star to be superstitious about adverse omens.

This evening for the first time the two men discussed what immediate measures they would take once they had seized power. They decided that the three Provisional Consuls would be Sieyès, Roger-Ducos, and Bonaparte and that the Council of Ancients and the Five Hundred would be suspended for three months while Sieyès put the finishing touches to his Constitution.

This same night the poet Arnault, Roederer, and Régnault, all of whom were in the conspiracy, were at Talleyrand's house in the Rue Taitbout, waiting to hear whether the *coup* would begin the next morning. When no word had come late in the evening, Arnault was sent to the Rue de la Victoire to reconnoitre. He found Josephine's salon filled with Jacobins, royalists, soldiers, politicians, and savants from the Institute. Gohier was staying close to his hostess, his infatuation evident for all to see, but Bonaparte did not appear to mind. Shortly after Arnault arrived, Fouché came in, looked blankly around him to see who was there, and glided over to pay his compliments to Josephine.

" Well, citizen Minister," said Gohier with the bluff, genial air of the President of France speaking to one of his trusted subordinates, " and what's the latest news?"

" News?" said Fouché. " There's no news. Just rumours."

" About what?" asked Gohier.

" Oh," said Fouché, " rumours about the conspiracy."

Josephine gave a little feminine cry, and Gohier patted her hand. He shrugged as though to dismiss such fantastic notions.

" Oh, I know just how much to believe," said Fouché. " I know my job, citizen Director. Have no fear. I will not be hoodwinked. If there had been a conspiracy, we should have revealed it on the Place de la Révolution or on the plain of Grenelle."

Fouché laughed aloud, as he often did at any reference to executions.

Josephine shuddered—delightfully, Gohier thought—and rebuked the Minister of Police. " How can you joke about such things?"

Gohier patted her hand again. " The Minister sounds as though he knows what he is doing. Don't be distressed, citizeness. When Fouché talks like that in front of the ladies you can be sure there is no need for him to carry out his threats. Be like the Government, citizeness. Don't worry about rumours. And don't let them spoil your sleep."

A pace or two away, General Bonaparte listened with an easy, watchful smile.

When Arnault managed to have a private word with Bonaparte he was told that the *coup* would be postponed until the 18th Brumaire.* Arnault pointed out that delay might be dangerous. Paris was already buzzing with rumours; the Minister of War had been informed of the whole plot; if the Council of Ancients took too long to make up their minds they might spoil everything.

Bonaparte replied: " I am giving them time to realize that I can do without them what I would rather do with them. It will be on the 18th."

After Arnault returned to Talleyrand's and reported on the postponement, he and Régnault went to the Faubourg St Germain to correct the proofs of the proclamation that was to be posted up and the pamphlets that were to be distributed on the day of the *coup*. Both men were nervous as they made their way through the silent streets. During the Terror this district had been almost as Jacobin as the Faubourg St Antoine, and any of the darkened houses or black alleyways might conceal enemies.

---

* 9th November

When they met a police patrol in the Rue Dauphine they wondered whether Fouché was even now rounding up the conspirators in their homes. It would be just like Fouché to hold his hand
until the last moment and then strike suddenly in the small hours
of the morning. Perhaps his conversation with Josephine and
Gohier tonight had not been jest after all?

*   *   *

If some of the lesser conspirators were inclined to be edgy
during these last days, Sieyès was positively miserable with apprehension. But this did not prevent him from making his own
private preparations for becoming head of the state. Every morning he was to be seen in the Luxembourg Gardens taking riding
lessons. General Bonaparte was not going to be the only man on
horseback on the day when history was made. Sieyès' horseman-
ship was not good, and the crowds of Parisians who gathered to
watch him found the spectacle irresistibly funny. Gohier and
Moulin also laughed immoderately when they heard about it.

On 17th Brumaire the General entertained Bernadotte, Jourdan and Bourrienne at dinner, but since the conversation was all
on the subject of war, and politics were not mentioned, the evening passed off pleasantly. That same night in the Hôtel de Breteuil
at a secret meeting of the conspirators, Lemercier received his
final instructions.[56]

The night before the *coup* was filled with last minute deceptions.
Gohier and Moulin had been completely taken in, and although
they believed it quite possible that Sieyès was attempting something against the Government, they were confident that their
friend General Bonaparte would be able to stop it easily. Josephine was forever sending little notes to Gohier, and on the evening of the 17th Brumaire she sent Eugene to deliver a special one
by hand. It was an invitation for the President to breakfast with
her at eight o'clock the next morning—this in spite of the fact
that she and the General had already promised to dine at Gohier's

that evening. Josephine wrote that she hoped Gohier would come to breakfast because " I have some very important things to communicate to you."[57]

After dinner that night when Bernadotte and Jourdan had left, Bonaparte took Bourrienne aside.

" I saw Barras this morning, he said, and left him much disturbed. He asked me to return and visit him tonight. I promised to do so, but I shall not go. Tomorrow it will all be over. But there is little time, since he expects me at eleven o'clock tonight. You must therefore take my carriage, go there, send in my name, and then enter yourself. Tell him that a severe headache confines me to my bed, but that I will be with him without fail tomorrow. Tell him not to be alarmed, because everything will soon be all right again. Evade his questions as much as possible. Do not stay long, and come to me on your return."

Bourrienne reached the Luxembourg sharp at eleven o'clock and made his way through the dark, empty corridors until he reached Barras' apartments. He sent in the General's name as he had been instructed to do, and was admitted at once. When Barras saw Bourrienne enter instead of Bonaparte his face fell. Bourrienne delivered the message, but when he rose to leave Barras said:

" I see that Bonaparte is deceiving me. He will not come again."

Bourrienne assured the Director that the General would certainly come the next day, but Barras only shook his head in disbelief.

Bonaparte seemed to be greatly pleased when his secretary returned at one o'clock on the morning of the 18th Brumaire to report this conversation.[58]

Brother Joseph was also assigned to duty on the eve of the *coup*. His task was to keep an eye on his brother-in-law, Bernadotte, and he performed it conscientiously. He and Bernadotte sat up together all night before setting off in the morning for the Rue de la Victoire.[59]

By now, only twenty-three days after the General had arrived in Paris, all possible preparations for the *coup d'état* had been completed. Berthier, Murat, Marmont and Lannes had done their work well; the regular troops could be counted upon. Some forty adjutants of the National Guard were Bonaparte's supporters, having been appointed by him after 13th Vendémiaire. Most of the officers of the Guards of the Councils and the Directory had been seduced from their parliamentary loyalty, and apart from the three Jacobin generals, most of the general officers in the Paris area had agreed to cooperate. Talleyrand had brought in General Beurnonville and General Macdonald; and only old General Lefèbvre, the honest, simple commandant of Paris, had not been forewarned of the plot.[60]

The plan of the *coup* was almost identical with that settled upon by Sieyès and Lucien on 29th September. Emergency meetings of the Council of Ancients and the Council of Five Hundred were called for seven o'clock and eleven o'clock the following morning, but notification of the meetings were sent only to those deputies who were in the conspiracy. The docile majority of the Ancients would be told that a Jacobin uprising was imminent and that to forestall it both Councils would have to be removed to St Cloud, out of reach of the Paris mob. The Council of Ancients would give General Bonaparte the command of the 17th Military District, including the Paris division of the National Guard. This appointment, in fact, was unconstitutional, but the wording of the Constitution of the Year III could conceivably be twisted to cover the case. Sieyès and Roger-Ducos would resign from the Directory, and the resignations of the other three Directors would be obtained somehow. The Councils would then appoint a Provisional Government of three consuls—Sieyès, Roger-Ducos, and Bonaparte—and would adjourn for three months while a new constitution was drawn up. General Bonaparte, entering politics for the first time, would be invited to take the oath of allegiance in the midst of the Councils.

All the night of 17th/18th Brumaire the Commission of the Council of Ancients, presided over by Cornet, worked behind closed shutters and drawn blinds to draw up the necessary decrees so that the Council would only have to vote on them on the morrow.[61] Roederer and Talleyrand wrote out the letter of resignation Barras was to be induced to sign the next morning. Nothing more could be done until the morrow. Early on the morning of the 18th Brumaire the lights were at last turned off in the little house in the Rue de la Victoire, and the General went to bed.

PART THREE

The Coup d'Etat

AFTER THE long November night, the morning of 18th Brumaire broke cold and grey over Paris. Little patches of fog were still drifting about the streets and clinging to trees and shrubbery when Napoleon's secretary arrived at No. 6 Rue de la Victoire at seven o'clock.

Bourrienne found a considerable crowd of officers already there before him—so many in fact that the little house could not hold them all. They paced in pairs up and down the cobbled garden paths, their sabres clanking on the stones and their spurs jingling when they turned. Every regiment in Paris was represented— big heavy-set dragoons in blue coats and white trousers, tall Grenadiers in bearskins, artillery officers in frocked jackets and plumed shakos, *chasseurs à cheval* in green tunics, lancers all in scarlet, infantry of the line in green, and general officers resplendent in gold lace and cocked hats decorated with tri-coloured plumes. Many of them were veterans of the Army of Italy, but the forty adjutants of the Paris division of the National Guard had also put in an appearance. Bourrienne was the only member of the General's entourage who had turned up in civilian clothes.

Josephine's drawing-room was full of officers. So was the garden, and the street in front of the house. As each new arrival dismounted and tethered his horse in one of the nearby avenues, he was shown in to the little oval dining-room of the General's home,

and there Bonaparte had a few brief words with him, congratu-
lating him in advance on the part he was to play in the day's
events.

Bourrienne went directly in to his master. Although the General
was rarely out of bed so early in the morning, his secretary now
found him fully dressed in his green coat and biscuit-coloured
breeches. Bonaparte was as calm as on the morning of a battle,
his olive face impassive and his blue-grey eyes cold and hard. This
unnatural stillness was something that he could usually summon
up at will in moments of great crisis. It was as though he
detached himself entirely from his emotions and lived for the
time being by his intellect alone.

In a corner of the room, little Berthier, in all things the perfect
Chief of Staff, provided an eloquent contrast to his General's
imperturbability. This morning he was fidgeting about nervously
and biting his nails. If Berthier had had no other purpose in the
room, it would have been worth the General's while to keep him
there to highlight his own composure.

Soon after seven o'clock General Lefèbvre, the Commandant
of the 17th Military District and Military Governor of Paris,
arrived in the Rue de la Victoire François Lefèbvre was no longer
a young man, as most of the revolutionary generals counted age.
When the mob had stormed the Bastille, he had been a sergeant-
major with fifteen years' service, happily married to a char-
woman. He was a big, gruff man with a long chin and a flat open
face that looked stupid. General Lefèbvre did not belie his looks,
for although he was good-hearted and very brave, he would
never had risen above sergeant-major except in the incredible
topsy-turvy world of the Revolution. On 18th Brumaire, after
twenty-six years of soldiering, Lefèbvre knew no more than any
private soldier about the political causes that led him into action.

He had heard that something unusual was happening in Paris
today and, although he was by no means clear in his mind as to
what it might be or how the army was involved, he had thought it
his duty to find out. As he rode to Bonaparte's house, he had

been puzzled to see so many troops marching through Paris without his orders, and he was quite flabbergasted by the sight of so many officers in the General's garden. When he was ushered in to Bonaparte, Lefèbvre was really quite angry.

He looked the General full in the face and in his thick Alsatian accent demanded: "What in hell is going on here?"

Bonaparte soon took care of this. He explained to Lefèbvre that France was in grave danger. Hostile armies were pressing in upon all the frontiers and the good soldiers who could save the Republic were prevented from doing so by a pack of lawyers who were making their fortunes out of the country's calamities.

Lefèbvre had heard something of this sort before, but never so clearly expressed. Bonaparte reached out and grasped him by the shoulder.

"Now then, Lefèbvre," he said, "you are one of the pillars of the Republic. Are you going to let it perish at the hands of these advocates? Join me in helping to save our beloved Republic. Look, here is the sword I carried with me at the Battle of the Pyramids." With this Bonaparte unclasped the scimitar he was wearing—he seemed to have a good supply of these Turkish weapons—and pressed it into Lefèbvre's hands. "I give it to you as a token of my esteem and confidence."

General Lefèbvre was not one of the world's great thinkers, but no one could ever accuse him of not being a true patriot. There were tears in his eyes when he accepted the proffered sword.

"I am ready," he declared, "to throw those buggers of lawyers into the river."

Bonaparte and the Commandant of Paris came out of the little room arm in arm and stood for a moment on the stone steps of the house where the crowd of officers could see them together.

Although it was the last thing to have crossed Lefèbvre's honest mind, he had just done himself the biggest favour of his military career. For the next fifteen years he was to follow the little General as trustingly and blindly as he had this morning, and in the process he was to become a Marshal of the Empire and

Duke of Danzig. He and his good wife, Catherine, were to mix on terms of equality with the nobility of Europe, but they never lost their fundamental simplicity. As time went by, Lefèbvre's stolidity even gave him some reputation as a man of common sense. And although people were inclined to laugh at his wife's habit of prefixing her reminiscences with the phrase. " When I used to take in the washing . . .," few couples in France were so well loved.*

On the morning of the *coup d'état* General Bonaparte was not yet certain that he commanded Lefèbvre's utmost loyalty, and consequently he took care to keep the old soldier close by his side all during the day. Bonaparte would not have understood it, but it was a needless precaution. Once Lefèbvre had given his word, he would have died rather than go back on it.

A few moments later Joseph Bonaparte and Bernadotte arrived together.[2] When Bourrienne saw that the Gascon general was in civilian dress he was startled into comment.

" General," he blurted out, " everyone here except you and me is in uniform."

Bernadotte looked down at the secretary in feigned surprise. " Why should I be in uniform?" he asked.

At that moment Bonaparte turned around, saw who it was, and stepped quickly over to the two men. " How is this? You're not in uniform! " the General said.

" I never am on a morning when I am not on duty," Bernadotte replied.

The cold eyes regarded him for a moment. " You will be on duty presently."

Bernadotte, who was to be on duty for many years to come, saw fit to disagree.

---

* There was, of course, some jealousy as well. Once, when an old acquaint-ance was obviously envious of his prosperity, title and style of living, Lefèbvre remarked : " Well now, you shall have it all, but at cost price. We will go down into the garden; I will fire at you sixty times, and then, if you are not killed, everything shall be yours."[1] Lefèbvre, who had been shot at a good deal oftener than sixty times, was actually offering his estate at con-siderably less than cost price, but nevertheless, the terms proved unaccept-able.

" I have not heard a word of it," he said. " I should have received my orders sooner."

Suddenly the impassive face which looked up at him so steadily relaxed and a smile of singular charm appeared on the hard features, although it did not touch the eyes. Bonaparte took Bernadotte's arm in a friendly gesture and led him into an adjoining room. There the General gave the recalcitrant Gascon three minutes of his time, explaining how the Directory was hated, the Constitution worn out, and the logic of events required a sweeping change.

" Go and put on your uniform," the General said. " I cannot wait for you long. You will find me at the Tuileries with the rest of our comrades."

Bernadotte betrayed his agitation by playing nervously with the hilt of his sword, but he steadfastly refused to take part in a rebellion.

Bonaparte then said: " All that I ask of you, General Bernadotte, is that you will give me your word of honour not to undertake anything against *me*."

It was an avenue of escape deliberately left open, a bolt-hole down which a proud man could get away with some vestige of dignity still left him. Bernadotte was wise enough to avail himself of it. He inclined his head. " Yes, as a citizen I will give my word of honour to remain quiet."

" What do you mean by that?" Bonaparte demanded.

" I mean that I will not go to the barracks or public places to work on the emotions of the soldiers and the people, but that if the Legislative Assembly and the Directory order me to defend them I will obey their orders."

The little man in front of him relaxed visibly.

" Oh, as to that I am well content. They will not employ you. They fear your ambition more than mine. I certainly have no other desire than to serve the Republic. I only wish to retire to Malmaison and live among my friends."

Bernadotte and the General then rejoined the others in the

dining-room. Shortly afterwards, Joseph led his brother-in-law off to breakfast at his house in the Rue Rocher where he could keep on eye on him.[3]

The other two Jacobin Generals, Jourdan and Augereau, did not make an appearance in the Rue de la Victoire, but Bonaparte was not seriously concerned by their absence. He was more disturbed to find that Gohier had not accepted Josephine's invitation to breakfast but had sent his wife instead.

Early that morning Gohier had at last become suspicious, partly because Josephine's breakfast invitation had been for so early an hour and partly because a number of unusual things seemed to be happening. He had been awakened, for instance, by the sound of troops forming up in the court of the Luxembourg. The tramp of feet, the rattle of muskets and the hoarse shouting of commands had brought him out of bed and over to the window.

When he had stuck his head out, he had seen General Jubé inspecting the full Guard of the Directory in the courtyard below. Gohier had leaned far out of the window in his nightgown and shouted to Jubé to ask what was going on. The commander of the Guard had shouted back that he was merely parading his troops prior to taking them on manoeuvres.

Gohier had come back from the window only temporarily satisfied. He could not quite believe that Josephine would lend herself to any political deception, but he decided not to go to Bonaparte's house that morning.

When Josephine told her husband that Gohier had sent his excuses, Bonaparte at once foresaw dangerous possibilities. He was afraid that the President, if he discovered in sufficient time that a *coup d'état* was taking place, might rally around him the Jacobin elements in the Assemblies and in the army.[4]

Dubois de Crancé, the Minister of War, would certainly have supported Gohier in this, and Bonaparte knew that de Crancé was already suspicious that a *coup* might be attempted on this day. At five o'clock that morning the Minister had sent an order to Colonel Sebastiani, instructing him to hold the 9th Dragoons in readiness. Sebastiani had signed the receipt for the order in silence and had then carried on with his part in the General's pre-arranged plan.

Bonaparte did not really believe that any effective opposition to the *coup* could be organized at such short notice, but nevertheless he was anxious to have Gohier where he could watch him.

" Have Madame Gohier write to him to come as quickly as possible," Bonaparte told his wife. " It is absolutely necessary that he be here."

At Josephine's urging, Madame Gohier actually did write a note to her husband, but we have no way of knowing what it contained. At all events, the President of the Directory took care not to place himself in Bonaparte's hands that morning.

*   *   *

Meanwhile, in the Tuileries on the right bank of the Seine, the Council of Ancients had gathered to pass the decrees which had been drawn up in secret the night before. The notice of meeting had been delivered to the representatives' homes only three hours before the time appointed for the session, and no notices had been sent to the Jacobin members.

Seven o'clock on a November morning is not the ideal time for the transaction of public business. The Tuileries was a magnificent old building which since the last years of Louis XV's reign had been the Parisian home of France's kings and the symbol of royalty, but at this hour it looked dark and neglected. The great Assembly Hall was cold, and when Cornet rose to speak in vague terms of a sinister plot that was threatening the Republic, the delegates, who were still a little sleepy and chilled by their early morning journey, heard him without enthusiasm.

Régnier, the delegate from Nancy, next mounted the tribune to propose that the Council be transferred to St Cloud where it could debate in calm and security and pass those laws necessary for the rejuvenation of the state. Régnier read out to the Council of the Ancients the text of the special decree:

The Council of Ancients by virtue of articles 102, 103 and 104 of the Constitution decree as follows:

Article 1: The Legislative Assembly is transferred to the commune of St Cloud. The two Councils will sit there in the wings of the Palace.

Article 2: They will meet there tomorrow, the 19th Brumaire, at noon. Any continuation of their functions and deliberations elsewhere is forbidden before that time.

Article 3: General Bonaparte is charged with the execution of the present decree; he will take all necessary measures for the security of the national representative bodies . . . [Here followed a list of the troops which were placed at the General's disposal.] General Bonaparte is called to the midst of the Council to receive there a copy of the present decree and to take the oath. He will act in concert with the Commission of Inspectors of the two Councils.

One or two delegates indicated their desire to debate so unusual a proceeding, but they were overruled by the majority of the Council of Ancients who knew what was going on. The special decree was voted into effect without discussion. The Council then adopted the prepared text of an Address to the French People, which purported to explain the measures taken.

*   *   *

Fouché was still doing his best to maintain contact with both sides. Between eight and nine o'clock he had taken his coach, first to the Tuileries where he had learned that the decree had been passed, and then to the Luxembourg where he sought out Gohier to tell him what the Council of Ancients had just done.

By now Gohier was definitely alarmed, and he looked at Fouché suspiciously. "I am astonished," he said, "that the Minister of Police should transform himself in this manner into a messenger for the Council of Ancients."

"I thought it my duty to let you know of so important a resolution," Fouché replied gravely. "And at the same time, I believed it proper to come to receive the orders of the Directory."

Gohier, however, was no longer so easily taken in by Fouché's explanations.

"It was even more your duty," he said angrily, "not to let us ignore the criminal intrigues which brought about such a resolution."

Fouché, his face impassive and his eyes as blank as glass, quietly defended himself by pointing out that the Directors had never wished to believe his warnings and that he had been forced to try to serve them by devious ways. Some of the Directors themselves, he said, had known in advance about the transference of the Councils to St Cloud, and he told Gohier that Sieyès and Roger-Ducos were even then closeted with the Commission of Inspectors of the Council of Ancients.[5]

This was true. Sieyès had waited at the Luxembourg as long as he dared for the escort of grenadiers he had understood would be furnished him. He had intended to ride to the Tuileries at the head of these troops so that Bonaparte would not appear to be the only one of the conspirators who commanded the allegiance of the army. It had been for this that he had so patiently endured those terrible riding lessons in the gardens of the Luxembourg.

At last, however, Sieyès had realized that he would get no military escort that day. Rather forlornly, he and Roger-Ducos had climbed into a carriage and driven off to the Tuileries just like any other civilians.

When Fouché left the Luxembourg, he went straight to the Rue de la Victoire. He was kept waiting a few minutes before being shown in to Bonaparte, but if this annoyed him he gave no sign of it. Fouché told the General that he had been to the Tuileries and that the decree had been passed, but he neglected to mention his visit to the President of the Directory.

He made up for this omission by protesting his devotion and zeal for Bonaparte's cause. Paris, he said, had already been sealed off. As Minister of Police, he had that morning ordered all the gates of the city closed and had stopped the departure of couriers and mails.

The General was not pleased by this intelligence. If he had wanted Paris isolated, he would have arranged it himself. As it was, Fouché's action carried far too many connotations of violence and illegality. Bonaparte thanked Fouché politely for his concern, but countermanded the order.

" All that is useless," he said. " The number of citizens and brave men around me must sufficiently convince everyone that I am with and for the nation. I shall take care to cause the decree of the Council to be respected and to maintain public tranquillity."[6]

*   *   *

While all this was going on, Barras was getting out of bed and taking a leisurely bath. Earlier that morning he had been awakened by an aide-de-camp who had informed him that the customary guards around the Luxembourg had disappeared. Barras was therefore inclined to be thoughtful as he splashed about in the water.

While he was still in the tub he had his first visitor of the day. Looking very tall and elegant, the black-haired Madame Tallien swept into his apartment. She brushed aside the protestations of one of the young aides-de-camp and went straight into the bathroom. There she told her former lover that Bonaparte had acted without him.

Barras was not surprised by the news, but he was shaken to find his fears receiving such rapid confirmation. As soon as

Madame Tallien had gone, he sent his confidential secretary, Bottot, to present his compliments to the General and ask how he could help him.[7] This done, Barras lay back in the warm water to indulge in a little quiet worrying, but he was soon interrupted again.

This time it was Gohier who descended upon him to pour out his suspicions that a *coup d'état* was actually taking place. Barras gravely agreed with the President and advised him to pick up Moulin and go to the Directors' conference room in the Tuileries where he would join them as soon as he was dressed.

Barras had time to do no more than get out of the tub and put on his dressing-gown, when he had his third visit of the morning. When he opened the door of his bedroom he found Talleyrand and Admiral Bruix awaiting him. The black-coated little diplomat limped across the room to greet him. Then, leaning on his cane and smiling sweetly, Talleyrand presented Barras with a copy of his resignation to sign.

As Barras read the document through, Talleyrand began to talk gently, with the slight lisp that always marked his speech. He pointed out that the Director was really in a very dangerous position. General Bonaparte controlled all the military forces in the capital—some seven thousand men—and he was not one who would treat his opponents lightly. Barras, in fact, stood in actual danger of his life.

Bonaparte had instructed Talleyrand to offer Barras a substantial bribe, if he should prove difficult. Years later the Director, with utterly unconvincing moral indignation, denied that Talleyrand and Bruix had so much as mentioned money to him. " They would not have dared," he declared. Barras, however, went on to add that if Bonaparte *had* intended to bribe him, Talleyrand must have pocketed the money himself. This, indeed, is exactly what happened. By the time Talleyrand had finished talking, Barras was far too frightened to raise any objections. He signed his resignation without protest, and Talleyrand limped out, richer by several hundred thousand francs.

In exchange for his resignation, Talleyrand had promised Barras safety for his life and property. The only condition made had been that the ex-Director should immediately leave Paris for his estate at Grosbois, where he would be free to pursue his peculiar hobbies undisturbed. To make sure that he reached Grosbois safely, and that he went directly there, the General had thoughtfully provided a cavalry escort which was even now waiting outside the Luxembourg.

*   *   *

At ten o'clock in the morning the inspectors, Cornet and Baraillon, at last arrived at the General's house with a finely uniformed messenger of state who carried a copy of the Council of Ancients' decree. Bonaparte received them at once, read through the decree and then coolly sat down and made a slight amendment to it. Bonaparte altered the document to give himself control of the two thousand Guards of the Directory as well as the regular troops of the 17th Military District.

Having completed this act of forgery, Bonaparte went out to the front steps of his house. Just as he emerged from the door, a rift appeared in the grey clouds overhead and a little pale sunshine broke through. Scarcely anyone especially remarked it at the time, but a few years later, when everything about this man was a cause for wonder, this stray sunshine was remembered as an omen and compared with the bright sun which broke through the December mists at Austerlitz.

The General waved the decree in the air for silence and then read it aloud. When he was finished, every officer present in the garden knew that there was some legal basis for what they were about to do. Bonaparte then spoke briefly about the perils of France and demanded of the assembled officers whether he could count on them in this hour of danger. The officers replied enthusiastically, shouting and brandishing their swords.

The forty adjutants of the National Guard were sent back to

their districts to keep an eye on the populace, but the rest of the officers were invited to accompany Bonaparte to the Council of Ancients. A big black horse was brought forth for the General, who mounted and led the way across the courtyard, down the long flagged passageway, and out through the carriage entrance into the street. Behind him came his glittering staff and a great cavalcade of officers.

As a result of this day's work, those who followed General Bonaparte this morning from the Rue de la Victoire to the Tuileries were, in the next fifteen years, to ride behind him as conquerors to all the major capitals of the Continent.

The General sent his stepson Eugene on ahead to inform the Council of Ancients that he had received their decree and would shortly be arriving to take the oath. In later years, Eugene remembered that while the Republic was being overthrown, his greatest concern was that for the first time in his life he would have to make a speech in public.[8]

At the same time, Bonaparte's aide-de-camp, Duroc, was sent galloping off to Marmont's little house in the Rue Saint Lazare. On the General's instructions, Marmont was holding a breakfast party for a group of officers who were to be induced to support the *coup d'état*. Lannes and Murat were also there, watching each other with mutual hostility. As usual, Murat was clothed in an almost comical splendour and Lannes, still on his crutches, was looking somewhat quaint and old-fashioned with his long, powdered hair which he refused to cut in the new style.[9]

Duroc burst into the room and addressed himself to Marmont.

" General," he said, a little breathlessly, " General Bonaparte has mounted his horse. He is going by way of the Pont Tournant. He told me to bring you orders to join him there."

The moment so eagerly awaited by the young generals from Egypt had arrived. Marmont stood ·up at the head of the table and formally asked his guests to join him in the adventure of overthrowing the Government. Several of the officers who had come to the Rue Saint Lazare on foot objected that they had no horses, but Marmont promptly despatched his servants to impress eight mounts from a nearby riding stable. Of all those present only General Allix and one other refused to throw in their lot with Bonaparte. The rest crowded outside to their horses, mounted and rode off to meet the General on the Boulevard de la Madeleine.[10]

Marmont, Murat and Lannes joined Berthier, Lefèbvre, Andréossy, and Macdonald near the head of the procession. By now the streets were lined with people curious to see what was going on. In the Place de la Concorde the crowd sent up a spontaneous cheer for the little General who looked so slight and plain in contrast with his brilliantly uniformed followers. Some of the crowd already had in their hands copies of the pamphlet Roederer had written to explain Bonaparte's version of the day's events.

A little further along the route Sebastiani's 9th Regiment of Dragoons was drawn up in review order, looking very smart in their blue coats and white mantles. Bonaparte took their salute, and then Sebastiani's troopers turned their horses into column and fell in with the cavalcade. At the Tuileries a second cavalry regiment had already taken up its position, and as the General dismounted to make his way into the Council Hall, still a third regiment began to file into the Tuileries Gardens by way of the Place Louis XV.

It was now a few minutes before eleven o'clock. The watery sun had dispelled the greyness of the day and touched with faint gold the warm grey stones of the Tuileries. The open parklands of the Champs d'Elysées stretching away to the west gave a pleasantly pastoral touch to the scene. On the Rue St Honoré, in the Tuileries Gardens, and in all the nearby streets, groups of civilians clustered around to watch the mustering of the soldiers. They watched it tranquilly and without the least sign of agitation.

General Bonaparte entered the Hall of the Council of Ancients, followed by his military entourage. He had prepared a short speech for the occasion and, after the President, Lemercier, had introduced him to the Assembly, he delivered it in a firm voice. Some of those who heard him, however, noticed that his Corsican accent was more pronounced than usual, that he appeared nervous, and that he spoke with stiff lips. The speech itself was quite suitable for the occasion:

> Citizens and Representatives, the Republic is perishing. You realise this and your decree will save it. Evil to those who wish for trouble and disorder. I will arrest them, aided by General Lefèbvre, by General Berthier and by all my companions-in-arms.
>
> Do not look in the past for examples which can retard your advance. Nothing in history resembles the end of the 18th Century, and nothing at the end of the 18th Century resembles the present moment.
>
> Your wisdom has produced this decree; our arms will see that it is executed.
>
> We desire a Republic founded on true liberty, on civil liberty, on national representation. We will have it. I swear it in my name and in that of my companions-in-arms.[11]*

As the General ended his speech, the elected representatives broke into a brief ripple of applause, but their hand-clapping was drowned out by the deep voices of the soldier spectators who were packed in the public galleries. As one man they shouted their affirmation of the promise the General had made in their name—
" We swear it! "

---

* *Citoyens représentans, la République périssait; vous l'avez su et votre décret vient de la sauver. Malheur à ceux qui voudraient le trouble et le désordre! Je les arrêterai, aidé du général Lefèbre, du général Berthier et de tous mes compagnons d'armes. Qu'on ne cherche point dans le passé des exemples qui pourraient retardes votre marche. Rien dans l'histoire ne ressemble à la fin du dix-huitième siècle, rien dans la fin du dix-huitième siècle au moment actuel. Votre sagisse a rendu ce décret; nos bras sauront l'exécuter. Nous voulons une république fondée sur la vraie liberté, sur la représentation nationale. Nous l'aurons . . . je le jure! je le jure en mon nom et en celui de mes compagnons d'armie!*

It was an impressive demonstration—too impressive for some members of the Council of Ancients who were visibly perturbed. This sort of dialogue between a General and his officers had little of democracy about it. Bonaparte then proceeded to take the oath of loyalty to the French Republic.

When the deputy Garat rose to point out that Bonaparte had not been asked to swear allegiance to the Constitution, Lemercier ruled him out of order on the grounds that the decree which had been passed earlier in the morning had specifically forbidden any debate before the Assemblies met again at St Cloud. A few representatives were inclined to dispute this ruling, but Lemercier quickly adjourned the session. The Council of Ancients then dispersed, their work for the day being done.

While this was going on, Lucien Bonaparte was presiding over a session of the Council of Five Hundred in the Palais Bourbon on the opposite side of the river. Again the Jacobin deputies had received no notice of the meeting, but the Five Hundred was a far less docile body than the Council of Ancients, and Lucien's announcement of adjournment was made over rising murmurs of protest. However, this Assembly also obediently dispersed, although to the accompaniment of loud shouts of " *Vive la Republique!*" and "*Vive la Constitution de l'an III!*" For the time being there was nothing the disgruntled deputies could do but wait for the morrow.

After a short interval in which he received the congratulations of his fellow conspirators, Bonaparte left the Tuileries to review some of the troops drawn up outside in the Gardens. The soldiers cheered him loudly and their officers waved their swords in the air to express their approval. Many of the members of the Council of Ancients who had come out to watch the inspection were further disconcerted by this display of soldierly zeal. The whole affair was beginning to assume a military rather than a parliamentary character, and the senators did not like it.

After the inspection Bonaparte found Barras' envoy, Bottot, waiting to speak to him. Bottot asked the General what Barras could do to be of assistance and Bonaparte replied, " Tell that man I do not wish to see him any more."[12]

Then, edging his big horse closer to Bottot so that the man had to back away, Bonaparte raised his voice and spoke loudly enough for the assembled soldiers to hear. As the General railed at Bottot, the horse kept moving forward, forcing the Director's secretary back step by step.

" What have you done with the France that I left in such glory?" Bonaparte shouted in evident anger. " I left peace, and I find war. I left victories, and I find defeats. I left millions from Italy, and I find despoiling laws and misery. Where are the one hundred thousand men who have disappeared from the soil of France? They are dead, and they were my companions-in-arms. This state of things cannot last. Within three years it would lead us to despotism."[13]

The effect of this noble anger was somewhat spoiled when at the end of his tirade Bonaparte lowered his voice and whispered that none of this was meant to apply to Barras.

And indeed, it was not. The poet, Arnault, had been busily recording the speech for the Paris newspapers. Those papers printed it enthusiastically the next day, but we now know that the address had been cribbed almost word for word from a letter sent to Bonaparte some days previously by the Jacobin Club of Grenoble.

After this dramatic confrontation with Bottot, the General went back inside the Tuileries where he met with the principal conspirators in the Hall of the Inspectors. With him were Sieyès, Roger-Ducos, and a number of the men who had been picked as ministers in the new government. Cambacérès, the Minister of Justice, chose this moment to begin fussing about legal technicalities.

" May I ask you, General, whether the Constitution is still the law of the land?" he inquired.

It was not the sort of question Bonaparte relished that morning.

" Why do you ask?" he demanded shortly.

Cambacérès explained that, as Minister of Justice, it was his duty to publish the decree of the Council of Ancients in the *Bulletin des Lois.* Unfortunately though, unless the decree was countersigned by the President of the Directory, it would not be legal.

Bonaparte looked at him witheringly.

" Lawyers! " he snorted.

Cambacérès made haste to modify his position. " I was speaking just now in my capacity of Minister of Justice," he said, " but I am speaking now as one who wants to help you. Since Gohier is not here, we may, I think, consider that his predecessor in the Presidency, Sieyès, is acting in his place. If Sieyès signs the decree, I'll see that it is properly published."

The General looked steadily at Cambacérès for a moment but did not deign to reply.

By now Gohier and Moulin had arrived at the Tuileries and were waiting in the Hall of the Directory for Barras, who was already on his way to Grosbois. The two Directors by themselves did not even constitute a quorum, so there was little they could do.

Dubois de Crancé, the Minister of War, had already begged them to issue warrants for the arrest of Bonaparte, Talleyrand, Murat and various other conspirators. De Crancé had promised that he would personally see to it that the arrests were effected, even, if necessary, on the road to St Cloud. Gohier and Moulin had listened sympathetically and had been about to sign the warrants when Lagarde, the principal secretary of the Directory and one of the conspirators, declared that he would not countersign any decree which did not have the sanction of at least three Directors. Legally, Lagarde was perfectly right, and Gohier and Moulin, who had a great respect for legality, had promptly abandoned the idea of arresting Bonaparte. Gohier even found some comfort in a legal quibble.

" At the worst," he said, " how can there be any revolution at

St Cloud? As President, I have here in my possession the seal of the Republic."

Moulin brightened up at this and added that, since Bonaparte was in any case going to dine at Gohier's that night, they would soon discover his real intentions.[14]

While the two Directors sat disconsolately in the Tuileries, Bottot came up to them with a copy of Barras' resignation. He was still somewhat shaken by his recent encounter with Bonaparte and very willing to pour out his story of how the General had stormed against the Directors. Gohier and Moulin listened to him with increasing apprehension. This was far worse than they had thought. They determined to seek out Bonaparte at once.

The General greeted them cordially when they appeared in the Hall of the Inspectors.

" I'm glad that you are falling in with the wishes of your two colleagues here," he said, indicating Sieyès and Roger-Ducos.

Gohier stiffly replied that he and Moulin were only obeying the law and had come to ratify the Council of Ancients' decree removing the two Chambers to St Cloud. He added that they were determined to defend the Constitution.

Bonaparte then made much the same speech to Gohier that he made earlier in the day to General Lefèbvre. The Republic was in danger and drastic steps would have to be taken to save it. Gohier, who was so justly known for his patriotism and republican zeal, would surely join them in saving France.

Indignantly, Gohier rejected the proposal. He upbraided Bonaparte for treachery, reminded him that he had engaged to dine at his house that night, and bluntly asked if he had accepted the invitation only to hide his hostile designs.

Still speaking gently, Bonaparte replied that he had no hostile designs. " But the Republic is in danger. And I shall save it. I *will* it."[15] He then suggested that Gohier and Moulin follow the example of the other three Directors and resign, but Gohier refused to be cajoled.

Bonaparte, finding that Gohier was adamant, then turned to

Moulin. " Sieyès and Roger-Ducos here have resigned. You are abandoned and isolated. Surely you won't refuse to sign your resignation?"

And now, for the first and last time, Moulin actually managed to say something for himself. He reminded Bonaparte that he had been a Republican general before he became a Director. " And a Republican General does not take the conduct of two deserters as a model."

Some of those present in the room did not have Bonaparte's patience. There were angry murmurs when they heard Moulin's reply, and the hot-headed Boulay de la Meurthe began to bluster that there were other, less gentle, methods of getting the resignations they required. The General, however, waved him into silence.

Just then—perhaps providentially, perhaps by design—a messenger was ushered in. He brought word that the Faubourg St Antoine was rising in arms at the instigation of Santerre the Brewer, the notorious revolutionary of 1792, who was commonly believed to be Moulin's illegitimate son. Bonaparte turned back to Moulin, addressing him for the first time by his military rank.

" General Moulin, are you Santerre's father?"

Moulin replied that he was not his father but that he was his friend.

Bonaparte glanced down at the message in his hand. " I hear that Santerre it trying to raise a mob in the Faubourg St Antoine. If he makes a move, I'll have him shot."

Moulin assured Bonaparte that the news could not be true, that Santerre was a discredited man who could no longer assemble four men around him. When Fouché spoke up as well to say that the city would remain quiet and that he would answer for the tranquillity of Paris, Bonaparte let the matter drop.[16]

Once it became apparent that nothing could induce Gohier and Moulin to resign, they were placed under arrest and sent back to the Luxembourg with an escort of three hundred soldiers commanded by General Moreau. The choice of Moreau for jailer was a shrewd one, because it did much to discredit the one man in France who might have been regarded as a military rival to Bonaparte. Moreau himself later realized that he had tarnished his reputation and was bitterly to regret the part he played on the 18th Brumaire.[17]

At the Luxembourg, Gohier and Moulin were separated and locked up under guard in different apartments. They were not allowed to communicate in any way with the outside world, and when some Jacobin members of the Five Hundred tried to visit them that afternoon they were turned away at bayonet point. Gohier, who was regarded as the more dangerous of the two, found that he had to sleep that night with a soldier sitting on the foot of his bed.

The two Directors passed the time in gloomy reflections. Gohier was especially bitter that Josephine had assisted in his betrayal. " How could I believe in such black perfidy?" he asked himself.[18] That night when darkness fell, Moulin made his escape from the Luxembourg by a window, but he had no further influence on the course of events.

*   *   *

The General's young men were set specific military tasks that afternoon. Lannes was given command of the infantry stationed about the Tuileries. Marmont was sent to the *Ecole Militaire* to keep in touch with the young officers there and see that they caused no trouble. Murat was despatched to St Cloud, Macdonald to Versailles, and Sérurier to Pont-du-Jour. Berthier and Lefèbvre remained by Bonaparte's side.

The General and the chiefs of the conspiracy spent the rest of the day in the Tuileries. Bonaparte was pleased, for the *coup* seemed to be going well. He did not yet realize how strong the opposition to him would be outside the circle of conspirators and loyal soldiers.

Josephine remained at home during the 18th Brumaire, but

after the departure of Bonaparte and his officers there was little for her to do except nervously await word on how the *coup* was progressing. Bourrienne stayed with her throughout the day, doing his best to keep up her spirits, although he was as anxious as she was. If the attack on the Directory turned out badly, not only Bonaparte himself but also all associated with him would certainly be treated very harshly indeed. The traditions of the Revolution, so concerned with humanity in the abstract, allowed no place for mercy in concrete political affairs. If the principal conspirators failed, they would undoubtedly be guillotined, and the best the others could hope for would be the " dry guillotine " of exile in Guiana. When Josephine and Bourrienne heard that General Moreau had quietly accepted Bonaparte as his legal military superior appointed by the Council of Ancients, they. were much relieved. Until then, Bourrienne, who was of a somewhat timid disposition, had not really believed that the *coup* could succeed.[19]

On 18th Brumaire the Bonaparte family made their headquarters in Joseph's house on the Rue Rocher. Joseph had not been able to keep Bernadotte under supervision for very long. Shortly after breakfast the Gascon general had gone off on his own to visit his Jacobin friends at various cafes. Joseph and his wife, Julie, stayed at home with Letizia, Lucien's wife Christine, and Pauline to wait for word of the *coup's* success or failure. In the afternoon Napoleon's mother was visited by her old friend, Madame Permon, and her daughter, Laura, the future Madame Junot.

When Madame Permon expressed her astonishment that Letizia had not been to see Josephine in such an emergency, Madame Bonaparte replied: " It is not to that quarter that I look for comfort. It is with Julie, with Christine. There, indeed, I find maternal happiness. But as for the other—no! no! " As she said this, Letizia compressed her lips and opened her eyes very wide in a characteristic grimace of emphasis.

Pauline Bonaparte was a strikingly beautiful woman, dark and

Emmanuel Joseph Sieyès
(1748–1836)

Jerome Bonaparte (1784–1860),
brother of Napoleon, created King
of Westphalia 1807 *(after Kinson)*

President of the Council of 500,
Lucien Bonaparte (1775–1840)

Letizia Bonaparte (1750–1836),
mother of Napoleon *(lithograph
by Delpech)*

Napoleon (1769–1821) *(Sketch by David in the Louvre)*

Josephine (1763–1814), Empress of France 1804–9 *(Prud'hon)*

Napoleon as 1st Consul presiding at the installation of the Council
of State, December 1799

Mme Récamier (1777–1849)

Joseph Bonaparte (1768–1844), elder brother of Napoleon, King of Naples
1806–8, King of Spain 1808–13

Charles Bernadotte (1763–1844), Marshal of the Empire and King of Sweden
(Charles XIV) 1818 (*Kinson at Versailles*)

vivacious, who at this time was married to General Leclerc. Her husband had gone with Murat to St Cloud, but Pauline seemed little worried by the crisis in the family's affairs. She spent the afternoon reclining on a divan in Joseph's drawing-room, admiring herself in a mirror.

Letizia, on the other hand, was extremely pale and nervous. She started up at the slightest sound and accompanied her conversation with convulsive gestures quite at variance with her usual air of calm dignity. She had three sons involved in the *coup* and all three would certainly be executed if it failed.

Madame Permon and Letizia were both Corsicans and had been friends since girlhood. This afternoon they passed the time in recalling the days of their youth, speaking as they always did in their native Italian. Letizia remembered how long ago on a hot August morning of 1769 she had gone to early morning mass in Ajaccio cathedral on the Feast of the Assumption of Our Lady. During the service she had been overtaken with the pains of childbirth and had hurried home to deliver Napoleon on a rug on the living-room floor of the old house on the Via Malerba. She spoke, too, of the days of her pregnancy, when she and her husband had hidden from the French soldiers on the wild slopes of Monte Rotondo and of how, only six years before, she had been forced to flee from Corsica, carrying her youngest child in her arms. The remembrance of past difficulties successfully surmounted is usually comforting, but today these reminiscences brought little pleasure. Letizia, who had known many crises in her life and much trouble, seemed to sense that whether this day's crisis turned out well or ill, it would bring tragedy to them all.

It was not until that evening when Lucien's valet, Mariani, arrived with word that all was going well that Letizia was somewhat reassured.[20]

For Caroline Bonaparte, at school at Madame Campan's outside Paris, the day passed like any other. She was a little petulant because she had not received a letter from Murat, but no news of the momentous events in the capital disturbed the calm of Madame Campan's classrooms.

*   *   *

In the Hall of the Inspectors, General Bonaparte and the military and civilian leaders of the conspiracy remained in consultation till late in the evening. Fouché noticed that two parties were already beginning to emerge among those who had joined forces to overthrow the Directory. Bonaparte, his brothers, and those soldiers who had been with him in Italy and Egypt were filled with the utmost confidence and insisted on carrying on according to plan. A number of the civilians, however, and especially those who were elected representatives, were already experiencing qualms. There were too many soldiers about, and it was becoming obvious that General Bonaparte would dominate the provisional Consulate.

Everyone had been anxious to get rid of the Directory, but the great majority of the conspirators were good republicans who abhorred the thought of a military dictatorship. Some of Bonaparte's officers, too, could scarcely conceal their impatience with the civilians. The General himself was careful not to give any such impression, but even he had grown curter and more commanding as the day wore on, while his officers seemed to regard all the talk of a new constitution as so much play-acting.

When some of the civilians complained to Fouché about this, he replied. " But it is done. The military power is in the hands of General Bonaparte. You yourselves invested him with it and you cannot now proceed a step without his sanction."[21] ·

A few of the civilian conspirators actually withdrew at this stage, but the majority felt that they were committed too deeply to draw back. They stayed talking and arguing among themselves late into the night. Bonaparte took little part in these discussions, and Roger-Ducos could think of nothing to say, but Sieyès bored everyone by droning on interminably about abstract themes that had no relation to the situation at hand. Many of the conspirators looked forward apprehensively to what might happen the next day when the Councils met at St. Cloud. All of them, however, were somewhat cheered when they learned that stocks on the Paris Bourse had actually risen that afternoon after word had got around that the Directory had resigned and that Gohier and Moulin were being held prisoner in the Luxembourg. Another encouraging sign was that at the Théâtre-Français that evening, the popular song, *le Chant du départ,* had been greeted with unusually prolonged applause by the ironic audience.

Amazingly, the only practical suggestion to be put forward that night came from Sieyès. He finally stopped discussing constitutional niceties and proposed that sixty of the Jacobin deputies be arrested in their beds. Bonaparte would not hear of it. He dismissed the idea as premature, and predicted that there would be neither resistance nor opposition.

" We will see about that tomorrow at St Cloud," Sieyès replied in a disgruntled tone.[22]

The General left his supporters well before midnight and returned home to the Rue de la Victoire. Political debate never held any fascination for him and he preferred to allow the others to discuss the policy of the new government by themselves. He said as much to Bourrienne that evening: " It is better to let them decide the matter, for by that means their vanity is flattered. I will obey orders which I myself have concerted."[23]

Long before this, Fouché had placards posted up about Paris exhorting the population to remain calm. This exhortation was scrupulously obeyed. Paris—the Paris of the Revolutionary tribunals, of the September massacres, of the sawdust basket; the Paris of the dead king, and the dead queen, and the little Dauphin dying in filth and madness in his prison—this Paris, who had killed so many of her inhabitants in the past ten years in the name of liberty, now seemed strangely apathetic on the night of the 18th Brumaire.

Among the bolder Republican spirits that night, there was

indeed some unco-ordinated activity. A few secret meetings were held by former members of the *Manège*, and some deputies of the Five Hundred tried without success to concert plans for the morrow. At one such meeting at Salicetti's house, Bernadotte suggested that when the Councils met at St Cloud a decree might be passed, giving him command of the two thousand grenadiers of the Guard of the Directory. His Jacobin friends were politely cool to the idea. General Bonaparte, they knew, could count on seven thousand well-armed regular troops, whereas the Guard of the Directory was little more than a force of gendarmes, well enough for parades and making a show on public occasions but hardly to be relied upon as a fighting force. In any case, the Jacobins saw little advantage in having two generals instead of one as a substitute for the Republic. It was late at night when Bernadotte and his friends left Salicetti's, and nothing had been decided, but Salicetti himself nevertheless thought he would be safer if he reported the whole thing to Fouché. He did so, but the Minister of Police rightly judged that no action was necessary.[24]

Bonaparte seems to have taken no special precautions to guard his house that night, although a small band of determined Jacobins, striking in the darkness at No. 6 Rue de la Victoire, could certainly have brushed the General's servants aside and murdered their master. With Bonaparte dead, the *coup d'état* would have collapsed completely, but no such attack transpired or apparently was even considered.

Before he went to bed, Bonaparte said to his secretary: " I am very well satisfied with my day's work. Goodnight, Bourrienne. We shall see what turns up tomorrow."[25] In spite of his confidence, however, the General slept that night with a brace of loaded pistols within his reach.[26]

*   *   *

The next morning, while it was still dark, trumpets and bugles all over Paris began to muster the regular regiments. After a hurried breakfast, the troops fell in on their parade grounds, were quickly inspected, then turned into column of route and set moving towards St Cloud. By eight o'clock the road from Paris to St Cloud was packed with carriages, officers on horseback, marching soldiers, deputies, functionaries, journalists and spectators. Pretty society ladies in their gayest dresses travelled with lunch-baskets and bottles of wine in their coaches, as though they were going to a picnic.

It had rained heavily during the night and the November air had a sharp bite to it. A strong wind stirred the bare branches of the trees along the road and sent a few grey clouds scudding across the sky. As the sun climbed higher, the misty air cleared and the landscape was lit with a pale autumn sunshine with no warmth in it. Overnight the season had changed. Yesterday's golden autumn had gone, and today winter was unmistakably on its way. But there is no record that the General or his supporters took this to be an omen. The sun-dial of Napoleon's superstition told only happy hours.

Bonaparte slept late this morning and was not ready to set out from Paris until nearly ten o'clock. A number of officers and some of the more important members of the conspiracy had gathered again at the Rue de la Victoire. A feeling of anxiety was evident among the General's friends this morning.

Cambacérès expressed the general disquiet: " Nothing has been settled yet. I am not too sure how it will all turn out."

The General tried to belittle his fears. " There are few men in the Councils," he said. " I listened to them all day yesterday. And how mean they were, and how basely self-interested! "[27] He radiated confidence and laughed at the gloomy faces about him. Once he spoke jestingly to a group of his generals: " Do you think there will be fighting today?"

Nevertheless, he refused to allow Josephine to accompany him, saying that the journey was not one for women. After a leisurely breakfast he climbed into his carriage and departed, accompanied by his staff on horseback and a troop of cavalry.

Near the head of the cavalcade Bourrienne rode alongside one of Bonaparte's aides-de-camp, Lavallette. As they were passing the Place Louis XV, where a guillotine had been set up during the Terror, Lavallette asked Bourrienne what he thought the outcome of the day would be. Bourrienne looked nervously out across the square and replied: " My friend, either we'll sleep tomorrow at the Luxembourg or we'll end up here."[28]

*   *   *

The imposing old castle of St Cloud stood on the slopes above the river and was approached by a narrow bridge and a long, tree-lined avenue that wound up the side of the hill.* The Gallery of Apollo, where the Council of Ancients was to meet, was a noble room, decorated in the classic manner by Mignard, and extending the full length of the right wing of the building on the first floor. The Five Hundred were to assemble in the Orangery, a long narrow annex overlooking the gardens. Despite its twelve tall windows that reached almost from floor to ceiling and took up most of one wall, the Orangery was a gloomy place. Its grandiose Corinthian columns and stuccoed cornices dated back to the spacious days of Louis XIV, but this morning the room was empty and barn-like. Although the great windows were bare and un-curtained, they let in only a grey November half-light. The hall was unheated except for an iron stove in one corner, and the chilled deputies who clustered around it could see their breath in the air. The Council Chambers were still not ready for use when Bonaparte arrived at St Cloud. Workmen were putting up decorations and laying carpets in the Gallery of Apollo, and carpenters were busy with hammers and saws, erecting benches in the Orangery.

As the General drove up, he was greeted by cheers and shouts of " *Vive Bonaparte!*", but some voices in the crowd also called out " *Vive la Constitution!*"

---

* St Cloud was destroyed by the Prussians in 1870.

Outside the palace, in the courtyards and gardens which were still wet from the previous night's rain, more deputies walked back and forth together, discussing the crisis. The delay in the opening of the Councils was the first serious setback to the conspirators' plan. As the deputies of the Five Hundred and the Council of Ancients mingled, they drew strength from each other, and the discomfort and indignity of their situation put them in a querulous mood. While they talked together in twos and threes, their opinion hardened. Those who had been excluded from yesterday's meetings protested loudly, charging that there was a conspiracy afoot against the Republic. Among the more moderate deputies, many disliked the high-handed way Lemercier and Lucien had dealt with the Assemblies and were apprehensive lest what they had thought would be no more than a reform of the Directory might end as a military dictatorship.

Whatever the people might think of them, the politicians of France had a good conceit of themselves. They were accustomed to deference, to special consideration. Why then were they being forced to meet in this unaccustomed place? And why were they surrounded by soldiers? There seemed to be soldiers everywhere. In the gardens the infantry regiments were standing easy, smoking and chatting together, and in the courtyards the 21st Chasseurs and the 8th and 9th Dragoons were dismounted and lolling about beside their horses.

Many of these soldiers were audibly speculating that they were there to overthrow the Government. The deputies could hear the insolent talk in the ranks. " It's time to get rid of these chatterers. While they've been quibbling, the army has been left without pay or shoes." And even more sinister: " Everything will be better when Bonaparte is master."

Only the Guards of the Directory were not openly hostile. These grenadiers were uncertain as to where their loyalty lay, and there was also some professional rivalry between them and the regular army. The Guards stood uncertain in the ranks and eyed Murat's dragoons without affection.

It was after one o'clock before the Orangery was ready. At last, however, the deputies filed in and took their places, their long scarlet togas and queer square birettas making a brilliant splash of colour in the bare, echoing room. Lucien Bonaparte, very young and handsome in his robes of office, declared the Assembly open. But he had no sooner spoken than the Orangery was filled with shouts of "Down with the dictator!", "*Vive la République!*", "*Vive la Constitution!*"

One of the delegates, Gaudin, a member of the conspiracy, at once suggested that a committee of enquiry be formed "in the name of the principles of the Revolution", and that until such a committee brought in its report all deliberation be suspended. This proposal drew a great roar of protest from the delegates, and the Jacobin Delbrel thereupon rose to demand why the Councils were meeting outside Paris, why there were so many soldiers outside the Council Chambers, and what substance there was to the tale of a plot against the Republic. Was it for this that France had undergone the sacrifices of the Revolution? Did anyone really believe that the French people wanted to live under the kind of Government that England had, or the United States? He then moved that each deputy individually be required to swear the oath of allegiance to the Constitution of the Year III. "We want the Constitution or death," he declaimed. "We will not be terrorized by bayonets. We are free here."

For a few minutes after Delbrel finished speaking, Lucien could not make himself heard. Five hundred deputies were on their feet, shouting, waving their arms in the air, and shaking their fists. When some semblance of calm was restored, another old Jacobin, Grandmaison, promptly seconded Delbrel's motion.[29]

Again Lucien vainly tried to restore order but was again shouted down. When at last he was able to put Delbrel's motion to the vote, the delegates overwhelmingly approved it. This was a serious error on the part of the Jacobins, who had nothing to gain by delay. They should at once have proceeded with their proper task of defending the Constitution and impeaching

Bonaparte. Instead, each deputy in turn now rose from his seat, made his way to the tribune, and repeated the oath.

In the first five minutes of the long drawn-out ceremony, only three men were sworn, and it looked for a time as though this procedure would take up more than the full day. The swearing-in was thereupon speeded up, but even so it was not completed until four o'clock. More than two hours were thus wasted. In this futile manner the first French Republic, which in one short decade had produced so much greatness and so much degradation, frittered away its final day. The sun was already low in the west when the last deputy had sworn his oath.

It is interesting to note too that when his turn came Lucien Bonaparte had no hesitation in quitting his seat on the rostrum to swear the oath of loyalty to the Constitution.

At two o'clock the Council of Ancients met in the Gallery of Apollo. They assembled much more sedately than the Five Hundred and listened quietly while their orchestra played *La Marseillaise*. As soon as Lemercier declared the session open, however, several delegates at once rose to their feet to demand an explanation of why the assemblies had been transferred to St Cloud. The Ancients were more dignified than the Five Hundred, but many of them were just as determined to discover the details of the alleged plot against the Republic. And those who had been excluded from the previous day's session were almost as angry as the Jacobin deputies of the lower house.

The halting explanations given by the chief conspirators in the Council of Ancients completely failed to satisfy the angry senators, and indeed only strengthened the suspicion that there was something to hide. Nearly an hour was taken up with futile debate before Cornudet raised a point of order. He pointed out that the decree of transference could not be considered legally executed until the two assemblies officially informed each other and the Directory of their presence in St Cloud. Until this formality was observed, Cornudet said, no business could legally be conducted.

Lemercier at once grasped the opportunity thus presented to him. He suspended the session while the formal notices were sent out to the Five Hundred and the Directory. Fifteen minutes later the Council of Ancients was reconvened to hear a message from Lagarde, the secretary of the Directory. Lagarde had returned the Council's notice with the statement that the Directory had ceased to exist. He reported—falsely—that four of the five Directors had resigned and that one of them, Gohier, was under police surveillance on the orders of General Bonaparte. In the hubbub that followed Lemercier again suspended the session while Lagarde's report was transmitted to the Five Hundred. At the same time the lower house was requested to prepare a list of nominees to the Directory so that the Council of Ancients could pick five men from that list, as the Constitution provided. This turn of events, which would have ruined the *coup d'état* had it been allowed to proceed unchecked, was communicated to General Bonaparte as soon as the session was suspended.

Bonaparte, meanwhile, was fretting in a nearby room on the first floor of the Palace. The room, which had formerly been one of Marie Antoinette's reception salons, was bare now and devoid of all furniture except for two armchairs drawn up before the huge ornate fireplace. The cold of the November day seeped in through the large windows facing the park and was not at all dispelled by the small fire that smoked and flickered in the grate. Sieyès, blue with cold and apprehension, sat huddled disconsolately over the fire. Since there were no fire-tongs, the ex-abbé kept poking at the smouldering wood with a damp log.

The General paced nervously up and down with a glow of excitement on his face. Every ten minutes Lavallette came into the room with a bulletin on how the Councils were getting on. The delay was beginning to tell on Bonaparte's nerves and every once in awhile he burst out with angry exclamations. According to General Thiébault, who visited him that afternoon, Bonaparte at one stage had a battalion commander summoned before him and railed against this unfortunate man for not obeying one of his orders. When the officer replied that he had followed the orders he had been given, the General cried out, " There are no orders here except mine! ", and instructed the officer to be arrested and thrown into prison. Thiébault, indignant at this injustice, made a formal protest and then drove back to Paris.[30]*

Just before four o'clock Bonaparte was further disturbed to see the Jacobin generals Augereau and Jourdan arrive. Both of them were deputies of the Council of Five Hundred, but they had not seen fit to attend the opening of the Assembly. At this stage of the affair, therefore, they had rather the air of vultures hovering hopefully about the body of one soon to die. Bonaparte rightly guessed that they had come to St Cloud because they had been told that the *coup* was going badly.

Augereau, a bold, crude man whose peasant manners and guttersnipe conversation would have prevented him from obtaining a commission in any army except that of the Revolution, swaggered in to confront his old Commander-in-Chief. He looked at Bonaparte with a sly smile and said: " Well, you're in a nice pickle now."

Bonaparte, however, was not to be outfaced by this blustering subordinate. Suddenly calm again, he looked at Augereau quietly and replied: " The wine is drawn, we must drink it. Be calm." And it was Augereau who dropped his eyes.

After the Jacobins had gone, Bonaparte turned to his brother Joseph and remarked, " He only came to sound me out."[31]

All this while, out by the main gate, a carriage and six horses stood waiting. They belonged to Sieyès and were his insurance against the failure of the *coup d'état*. The ex-abbé was determined that, whatever happened, he would survive the events of this day just as he had survived the Terror. Talleyrand had also made his own preparations for flight.

Shortly before four o'clock General Bonaparte was told that

---

* However, it is worthwhile noting that Thiébault did not tell this story until after Waterloo, and that no one else who was present at St Cloud that day mentions the incident.

the Council of Five Hundred had been asked to select nominees for a new Directory. He at once ordered a regiment of cavalry to be drawn up in review order in the courtyard. Then he announced to the officers around him that he was " going to make an end of it ". Bare-headed, with only Berthier and Bourrienne accompanying him, he crossed the Salon de Mars and made his way over to the Gallery of Apollo. On the way he met Arnault, who had just arrived from Paris.

Arnault stopped him. " General, I have seen Fouché."

" Well?" said Bonaparte.

" He thinks you should rush matters, that you could easily get bogged down with delays. This is also what many of your best friends believe. Talleyrand for one. They all say that there is no time to lose."

" No time will be lost," Bonaparte replied with a smile. " A little patience and all will be well."

Nevertheless, in spite of the General's confident words, Bourrienne noticed that he was pale and ill at ease and that he walked in a quick, angry way which betrayed his inner agitation and did not promise well for what he would have to say to the Council of Ancients. As a rule it would have been illegal for any outsider to enter the floor of the Assembly without invitation, but the sitting of the Council of Ancients was now suspended and the General could come in on the pretext of speaking to the President during the recess. Passing down the narrow aisle to the centre of the hall, Bonaparte approached the President's tribunal and stood with his back to the door at the left of the President.[32] As soon as word got around that the General had come to the hall, the delegates thronged back to their places.

While he stood there, looking at his red-robed audience, Bonaparte's nerve failed him. He had hoped for the same easy success he had achieved the day before and was disconcerted to find that he would now have to argue and discuss and give reasons for his actions. He was a man born to command, and he loved to do that for which he had been born, but he was at some disadvantage in the cut-and-thrust of open debate. No reliable text of his speech exists, but all who heard it are unanimous that the General stuttered and stammered and spoke incoherently. The next day the *Moniteur* presented an official version of the speech by piecing the fragments together to make a more or less coherent whole, but what the Council of Ancients actually heard was a very poor performance.

The General began by saying that the Republic was on a volcano, that he would speak to them " with the frankness of a soldier ", and that they should suspend judgment until they had heard what he had to say. But then, instead of revealing anything about the dangers he claimed were threatening the Republic, he abruptly broke off to mutter angrily that calumnies had been heaped upon him, that his enemies were calling him a new Cromwell and a new Caesar and were suggesting that he wished to establish a military dictatorship.

" If I had wished to destroy the liberty of my country, if I had wished to usurp supreme power, I need not have waited for the orders you gave me. I did not need the authority of the Senate. More than once, in extremely favourable circumstances, I have been called upon to take power. After our triumphs in Italy I was called by the wishes of the nation. I was called by the wishes of my comrades, by those soldiers who had been so badly treated when they were no longer under my orders, those soldiers who are still obliged today to wage a horrible war in the departments of the west."

Three-quarters of the Council of Ancients had in any case been the General's supporters, but as the Assembly listened to these wild ravings, delivered in an excited voice thick with a Corsican accent, murmurs began to be heard in the hall. Bonaparte was interrupted repeatedly by hecklers, an experience with which his military training had poorly equipped him to deal.

He repeated the falsehood that four of the five Directors had resigned and he announced that in the Vendée several localities had just fallen to the royalist insurgents.

"Let us avoid losing," he declaimed, "those two things for which we have made so many sacrifices—Liberty and Equality."

"And the Constitution?" demanded Lenglet of Arras.

The interruption caused Bonaparte to break off what he was saying. He stood for a moment as though undecided, then he raised his head and burst out with the only eloquent portion of his speech.

"The Constitution!" he exclaimed. "Is it proper for you to invoke it? You violated it on 18th Fructidor. You violated it on 22nd Floréal. You violated it on 30th Prairial.* The Constitution! The Constitution is invoked by all factions and has been violated by all. It is despised by all. The country can not be saved by the Constitution, because no one any longer respects it."[33]

All this was undeniably true, but the General neglected to say that, because Augereau had been no more than his emissary on 18th Fructidor, he himself bore the primary responsibility for setting the precedent by which Republican Governments could be overthrown by *coups d'état*.

This little spurt of eloquence was soon over, and the wild ramblings began again. "Representatives of the people, do not see in me a miserable intriguer who covers himself with a hypocritical mask ... Let us save equality and liberty ... I declare to you that, as soon as the dangers which have made it necessary to confer extraordinary powers on me have passed, I will abdicate those powers ..."

Interruptions were becoming more frequent now, however, and his audience was getting completely out of hand. Cornudet sought to take the General's part. He leapt to his feet and turned to face

---

* By the *coup d'état* of 18th Fructidor (4th September 1797) the Directors Barras, Rewbell and Larevellière-Lépeaux expelled their colleagues, Barthelémy and Carnot, forty-two members of the Five Hundred, and eleven of the Council of Ancients. General Augereau, as Bonaparte's emissary, provided the necessary force. By the *coup d'état* of 22nd Floréal of the Year VI (12th May 1798) the Five Hundred expelled Treilhard from the Directory and replaced him with Gohier, and by the *coup d'état* of 30th Prairial of the Year VII (18th June 1799) Merlin of Douai and Larevellière-Lépeaux were replaced on the Directory by Roger-Ducos and General Moulin.

the assembly. What more, he demanded, did they want to hear? General Bonaparte himself, to whom so many honours had been accorded, to whom the whole nation owed so much gratitude, the man before whom Europe and the entire world fell silent in admiration, this man had himself come before them and testified to the existence of a conspiracy against the Republic. What more did they want?

In answer, from various places in the Hall, delegates shouted out: "What are the names of the conspirators? Name them! Name them!"

At this, Bonaparte raised his voice to reply: "Very well, if I must give an explanation and if I must name men I will name them. I will tell you that Barras and Moulin proposed to me to be the leader of a party whose aim was the overthrow of all men holding liberal opinions."

This was really too much, even for the Council of Ancients. Everyone knew that Barras and Moulin were hardly on speaking terms, and this suggestion of a rightist plot was in flat contradiction to everything that had been said about a Jacobin conspiracy. Even the President, Lemercier, felt that he had to press the General to be more explicit. Instead of making any detailed defence of his accusations, however, Bonaparte merely repeated that the Constitution had been violated three times and was no longer any guarantee of the liberty of the citizens. "Different factions, he said, have come to ring at my door and offer me that power which I could accept only at the hands of the French people."

Worse was to follow. The General by now was completely beside himself and he went on to attack in the most violent terms the Council of the Five Hundred as men who were in the pay of the enemy, men who wished to see scaffolds set up again in the streets, and men who had sent emissaries to Paris to organize a rising.

The General's supporters were put completely out of countenance and sat listening to him in silent dismay. Bonaparte's voice now rose to a shout: "And if any orator in foreign pay talks about outlawry, let him beware of levelling such a decree against himself. At the first sign I should appeal to you, my brave companions-in-arms, to you Grenadiers whose caps I see yonder, to you brave soldiers whose bayonets are in sight. Remember that I go forward accompanied by the God of fortune and the God of war!"

With these insolent words, hostile murmurs could be heard throughout the Hall, and Lemercier made one more attempt to bring Bonaparte to his senses. "General," he said, "the Council invites you to reveal all you know of the plot by which the Republic is threatened."

This was quite beyond Bonaparte's power. All he could think of was to repeat his accusations against Barras and Moulin. He added, however, that they were no more guilty than many others because they expressed only what was universally desired.

"If Liberty perish," he shouted, "you will be responsible to the universe, to posterity, to France, and to your families."

Bourrienne and Berthier, in an agony of embarrassment, plucked the great man's coat-tails from behind, and Bourrienne whispered: "Withdraw, General, you do not know what you are saying!" Between them, Berthier and Bourrienne managed to edge the General down the aisle to the door. There Bonaparte paused, muttered a few incoherent words, then turned around for the last time to the assembly and shouted: "Let those who love me follow me!" While an aide-de-camp held aside the tapestry hanging over the door, the General was hustled out of the Hall.[34]

No one tried to prevent Bonaparte leaving. However, Bourrienne, believed that if, when the General had begun to retire, the President had said: "Grenadiers, let no one pass," Bonaparte would have ended his career on the Place de la Révolution instead of sleeping the next night in the Luxembourg. As it was, the docile majority of the Council of Ancients promptly passed a vote of confidence in their General.

As Bonaparte stepped outside the Gallery of Apollo he saw

Augereau standing nearby with an unpleasant smile on his face. If the *coup d'état* failed, there was every possibility that Augereau, Jourdan and Bernadotte would inherit the power, but the General thought it worthwhile to make one last appeal to his old divisional commander from the Army of Italy. Bonaparte always believed— and with good cause—in the magic of military comradeship, the pull of glory, and the names of great victories. Augereau had been with him on the bridge of Arcola in 1796, and it had been Augereau's troops who, late in the afternoon, had stormed across to win the day.

Now as he passed on the other side of the courtyard, Bonaparte called out: " Augereau, remember Arcola! "[35]

But none of the malice faded from Augereau's smile.

*   *   *

However, Bonaparte recovered quickly. (It was always wonderful how quickly that marvellous man could recover—he was to do so again at Marengo, and at Wagram, and after the Battle of the Nations at Leipzig—he was to do it, indeed, on St. Helena and create his own legend in the process.) In any case he recovered now. It has been suggested, with some plausibility, that it was the sound of the word ' Arcola ' and the memory of his own greatness that pulled him together. He dashed off a confident note to Josephine, sent Bourrienne off to Paris with it, then, tucking his little silver-tipped riding switch under his arm, he strode over to the Orangery, accompanied by four Grenadiers.[36]

The Council of Five Hundred, having finished swearing in each of its members, had again relapsed into disorder. Accusations were being tossed back and forth; a dozen or more deputies were on their feet simultaneously; and no speaker was willing to yield the floor to another. Bonaparte could hear the representatives shouting long before he reached the Orangery. Because the hall connecting the Five Hundred's meeting place with the main part of the palace was packed with spectators and hangers-on, the

General's escort of grenadiers had to shoulder their way through the crowd.

Bonaparte knew that the crisis of the day was approaching. There were too many Jacobin and regicide deputies in the Five Hundred for a peaceful transfer of authority. The men who had been responsible for killing the king and for the Terror felt that they could not afford, for their own safety's sake, to relinquish their parliamentary immunity. They knew that they had blood guilt upon them and believed that, if power passed to any other group in the state, they would be pursued by avengers. Bonaparte, in fact, had no intention of allowing vengeance in the new France he hoped to create, but the Jacobins could not be sure of this. As they saw it, they could do nothing but resist. This had been the General's fundamental miscalculation, but he had gone too far to turn back. Now he had to choose between the scaffold and the throne.[37]

Lucien had already read Barras' letter of resignation to the Assembly. Although it had been written by Roederer with Talleyrand's help, it expressed, better than Barras himself could have done, exactly what he would have wished to say upon retirement:

> Citizen President, Having entered into public affairs solely from my love of liberty, I consented to share the first magistracy of the State only that I might be able to defend it in danger; to protect against their enemies the patriots compromised in its cause; and to ensure to the defenders of their country that attention to their interests which no one was more calculated to feel than a citizen, long the witness of their heroic virtues, and always sensible to their wants.
>
> The glory which accompanies the return of the illustrious warrior to whom I had the honour of opening the path of glory, the striking marks of confidence given him by the legislative body, and the decree of the National Convention, convince me that, to whatever post he may henceforth be called, the dangers to liberty will be averted, and the interests of the army insured.
>
> I cheerfully return to the rank of a private citizen: happy, after

so many storms, to resign unimpaired, and even more glorious than ever, the destiny of the Republic, which has been, in part, committed to my care.[38]

This remarkable epistle caused a sensation in the Assembly. Some deputies called for it to be read a second time, perhaps because Lucien too had not lost his Corsican accent. Others demanded to be informed whether Barras' resignation as a Director was legal; still others suggested that nothing except the threat of physical violence could possibly have induced Barras to resign; and a third opinion had it that Barras was in secret collusion with General Bonaparte.

At that moment Bonaparte and the four grenadiers suddenly appeared in the doorway of the Orangery. The grenadiers halted at the threshold, but the General, uninvited, walked slowly down the aisle towards the President's rostrum. For an instant the storm of voices died down, only to rise again with renewed intensity.

" What! Bayonets here?" someone cried. Another shouted: " You are violating the sanctuary of the laws, withdraw immediately! " Destrem, a huge bear of a man, shambled menacingly forward and shouted: " Is it for this then that you became a conqueror?" And Bigonent roared out with rage: " Rash man, what are you doing?"[39]

A number of deputies rushed up to the General, shouting " Down with the dictator! " They aimed blows at him, and Destrem caught him by the collar of his coat and shook him. " So that's what your victories were for! " Destrem shouted angrily again and again as he pushed the little General to and fro. Another old Jacobin, Aréna, leaned over his colleagues' arms and struck at Bonaparte. Later the story was put about that Aréna and some other deputies had drawn poniards on the General, but no reliable witnesses could ever be found to support this. Up in the public galleries which were packed with spectators a woman cried out shrilly: " *Vive Bonaparte!*", and the cry was taken up by other voices. Down below, on the floor of the legislature, a dozen fistfights had broken out. Just as Bonaparte fell back fainting, deadly pale, with his head lolling to one side and blood on his cheek, the grenadiers intervened and dragged him from the Hall.

In fact, Bonaparte was rescued almost unscathed. Although the story that daggers had been drawn was told later in the most explicit detail, Bourrienne says that the General himself never mentioned it that day or in his account of the episode to Josephine in the early hours of the next morning.⁴⁰ One of the grenadiers, Thomé, whose coat had been ripped in the scuffle, was subsequently credited with having saved the General's life, and Josephine presented him with a sum of money for his alleged heroism. However, the best proof that no daggers were drawn is the fact that Bonaparte emerged virtually unharmed. He would certainly have been killed or wounded if poniards had been brought into play.

After the General had been dragged from the Hall, Lucien did his best to defend him. " You calumniate my brother in supposing him capable of entertaining any views hostile to liberty," Lucien declared. " On the contrary, no man has given more pledges to support it than he has. I have no doubt that he came into the assembly for the express purpose of making some important communication about public affairs."⁴¹ The shouting mob of representatives roared back that Bonaparte had tarnished his glory and was a disgrace to the Republic. Lucien retorted that he himself was personally as attached to liberty as any there.

In a dramatic bid to gain time, he temporarily resigned the Presidency to Chazal, mounted the tribune and begged that the General be allowed to reappear and that he be granted an orderly hearing. Instead, the deputies raised the shout of " *Hors la loi!*", the same cry that had signalled the end of Robespierre's rule, a cry that in former days had meant certain death.

Outside, a group of senior officers who were Bonaparte's supporters, heard the cry for outlawry go up in the Assembly, and all of them paled. Lucien took the chair again immediately after his short speech, but steadfastly refused to put the motion calling for the outlawing of his brother. When he saw that there was no possibility of bringing the Assembly under control, he beckoned General Frégeville and whispered a message in his ear for Bonaparte. " If the sitting is not interrupted in ten minutes, I cannot answer for the consequences."

Bonaparte had been badly shaken. Physically he was a small man who had been subjected to very rough handling. It was hardly surprising, therefore, that when he rejoined Sieyès in the ante-room he was almost incoherent. " They want to outlaw me," he muttered.

Sieyès looked up from where he was huddling over the fire and said: " They will themselves be outlawed then."

Bonaparte might be small, but he was also tough and wiry. In a very few minutes he had completely recovered his composure. Moreover, matters were at last back on a level he could understand. A senator called Fargues was sent to the Council of Ancients to inform them of the attack on the General they had appointed and to ask for the passing of a special decree which would give Bonaparte civil as well as military powers to restore order. But Bonaparte knew that it was not by such means that the affair would be decided. When General Frégeville brought Lucien's message to him he strode across to the window, opened it, and leaned out. His loyal troops in the courtyard below looked up to see their General, his uniform dishevelled and blood on his face, wave his sword at them and cry, " To arms! To arms! "

It was a cry that was not to be silenced again for sixteen years.

Bonaparte strode downstairs to the courtyard. Admiral Bruix's great black horse was brought out for him, and with some difficulty, for he was still weak from his manhandling in the Orangery, he mounted. The horse, frightened by the noise of the soldiers falling in and the uproar that was coming from the Council of Five Hundred, reared and almost threw him. When Bonaparte had brought his prancing mount under control, he first of all rode up to the grenadiers of the Guard of the Directory and began to harangue them.

" Soldiers," he demanded, " can I trust you?"

There was no evidence in their solemn faces that he could. These men had always been directly under the orders of the Assemblies; both self-interest and duty inclined them to support their legal masters. Sieyès, who preferred to watch this scene from the upstairs window, believed that he saw a suspiciously hostile movement in the ranks as though some of the grenadiers might reach out and seize the General. If this had ever been the intention, however, it came to nothing, for Bonaparte galloped away to the other side of the grounds where his loyal dragoons and infantry of the line gave him a mighty roar of welcome.

Nevertheless, time was passing. By now it was five o'clock and the dull November dusk was closing in. The bare trees in the park no longer cast shadows on the ground and the mists of night were already beginning to gather about their lower limbs. Inside the palace it was almost dark.

In the Orangery, Lucien made one final gesture of defiance. Facing the shouting deputies, he cried out: " What! Do you wish me to become the assassin of my brother? Never! I would rather tear off the magistral robes! " Dramatically he took off his cape, his scarlet robe, and sash, and placed them on the edge of the tribune. For a moment the deputies fell silent at the seriousness of what was being done. Some urged him to reconsider, but many others again took up the cry for his brother's blood. Just at that moment a party of grenadiers with fixed bayonets forced their way through the milling mob of representatives, formed up around Lucien, and escorted him out through the door as though—according to one of the spectators—he were a shrine.

When Lucien emerged from the Orangery he was pale and furious. Now, for a brief half hour, his anger was to raise him above himself and provide him with his single, dubious place in history. Although he genuinely believed himself a republican, he was to be instrumental in destroying the Republic. Later, after he quarrelled with Napoleon, Lucien was to regret the part he played in the *coup d'état*, and the regret may have been sincere.

Certainly, Lucien's only talents were those of the demagogue; he might well have made his mark in a democracy.

In any case he now realized better than anyone else that there was no time to lose. He quickly mounted a horse and rode over to his brother. The two Corsicans embraced, but it was the younger man who, as President of the Assembly, made the telling speech to the wavering grenadiers of the Guard.

" Citizen Soldiers," he declaimed, " I tell you as President of the Council of Five Hundred that the majority of that Council is at this moment held in terror by a few representatives of the people. These men are armed with stilettos. They surround the tribune. They menace their colleagues with death and utter the most atrocious threats."

The soldiers listened to Lucien doubtfully. Although he was President of the Five Hundred, he was also the brother of General Bonaparte, and they had heard the talk of a military dictatorship.

Lucien, sensing this, changed his plea.

" I declare to you that these brigands, who are undoubtedly in the pay of England, have risen in rebellion against the Council of Ancients. They have dared to talk of outlawing the General, who is charged with the execution of its decree, as if the word ' outlaw ' were still to be the death warrant of men most beloved by their country."

This was a clever appeal, for it sought to reassure the grenadiers as to the legality of the action demanded of them. As Lucien paused, he could sense the hesitation in the ranks, and he was quick to press home his advantage.

" I tell you that these madmen have outlawed themselves by their attempt upon the liberty of the Council. In the name of the people, who for so many years have been the victims of terrorism, I charge you with rescuing the majority of the representatives, so that delivered from poniards by bayonets, the representatives may deliberate on the fate of the Republic."

Lucien turned away from the silent ranks of grenadiers and

addressed himself for a moment to his brother, the regular troops, and the crowd of spectators.

" General, and you soldiers and you citizens, you will not acknowledge as legislators of France any except those who rally round me." Then, turning back to the grenadiers of the Guard, he went on: " As for these who remain in the Orangery, let them be expelled by force. They are not the representatives of the people but the representatives of the poniard. Let that be their title and let it follow them everywhere. Whenever they dare show themselves to the people, let every finger point at them every tongue name them by the well deserved title of representatives of the poniard.

" *Vive la République!* "[42]

It had been a good speech. Lucien was never to make a better one. But for all that, it had not entirely achieved its purpose. The grenadiers, whose duty it was to guard the Assembly, still hesitated. Lucien saw this and had an inspiration. He drew his sword scraping from its scabbard and urged his horse alongside the General's. Then, placing the tip of his sword against Bonaparte's breast, he cried out in a loud voice: " I swear that I will stab my own brother through the heart if he ever attempts anything against the liberty of Frenchmen! "

This theatrical touch was too much for the grenadiers. Their hesitation vanished and they shouted " *Vive Bonaparte!* " just as enthusiastically as though they had been veterans of the army of Italy.

General Bonaparte gave a short command, and Murat, who had been waiting fretfully for just this order, at once began to form a column of grenadiers. As the files fell in, the drummers were ordered to beat the charge. The troops were soon in column, looking taller than natural in their bearskins and very menacing as the half-light reflected dully from their naked bayonets. When Murat's column advanced, the drums began their impatient throbbing. The twilit park and courtyard filled with the sound, the terrible, exciting sound that had announced the presence of the

Revolution on so many battlefields. The noise swelled in volume as the marching troops neared the palace. Once inside the building, the beat of the drums grew louder and louder, reverberating down the empty rooms and corridors until it drowned out all other sounds.

The quarrelling deputies heard the drums and fell suddenly silent. On and on that wild music came, ever nearer and louder, as the Grenadiers marched in quick time towards the Orangery, the drums beating them forward. For a moment the column of soldiers hesitated at the door, as though instinctively aware that once they stepped over that threshold, France would never be the same again. Briefly the drums fell silent, and an officer cried out: "Representatives, withdraw! The general has ordered it!" Then as the drums again rolled louder to drown out the shouts of the deputies, the grenadiers entered the Assembly. Their muskets came down to the ready and their bayonets bristled and gleamed in the twilight.

Murat's voice rose above the uproar. "All right, lads. Throw these rascals out of the hall for me!" And the soldiers pushed forward eagerly to obey.

Most of the deputies fled. Some of them leapt from the windows in their haste to get away, and some struggled in a knot at the far end of the room as they tried to push through the too-narrow doors. A handful of the braver ones sat down, folded their arms, and prepared to die for the honour of the Republic. This final consolation was denied them. Instead of using their bayonets, the big grenadiers merely picked them up like naughty children, carried them over to the tall windows and contemptuously tossed them down into the garden below. In the shadowy grounds about the Palace of St Cloud, the last representatives of the First French Republic ran in panic, dodging helter-skelter across the garden in the deepening November dusk and leaving shreds and tatters of their crimson robes on the protruding branches of the orange trees.

That night a private citizen met one of the fleeing deputies in the garden and laughed full in his face. " The farce is played out," the citizen said with a scornful snap of his fingers, and the deputy disappeared.

*　　*　　*

At about this time Letizia Bonaparte and Pauline, with Madame Permon and her daughter, were at the Théâtre Feydeau, watching a performance of *l'Autre dans son Ménage*. Suddenly the play was interrupted and the announcement made that General Bonaparte had narrowly escaped assassination at St Cloud. Pauline shrieked so loudly that everyone in the theatre turned to look at the Bonaparte box, then she promptly went into hysterics. Letizia, whose own hand was shaking so badly she could scarcely hold the glass of water brought by the attendant, did her best to quieten her daughter. When Pauline's sobs at last died away, the party left the theatre and went to Lucien's house in the hope of hearing some reliable news.[43]

That evening, too, another member of the Bonaparte family was informed of the day's happenings. Madame Campan's school for girls had closed for the night and the young ladies were all safely in their beds when a thunderous knocking came at the heavy main door. When the concierge called out nervously to ask who was there, he received the reply: " Open up! We have a message from General Murat! "

When the chains were undone and the door opened, a sergeant of grenadiers and three privates were discovered on the threshold. The sergeant saluted.

" Message for Mademoiselle Caroline Bonaparte," he said, handing his letter over.

The concierge took it to Madame Campan who called Caroline to her study to receive it. For once the iron discipline of the school seems to have broken down, for Hortense Beauharnais, Josephine's daughter, and a little cluster of girls, all in their night-dresses, were waiting in the corridor for Caroline when she emerged from Madame Campan's study.

Caroline came out, waving the letter in her hand.

"The Directory is overthrown," she announced grandly. "Murat has thrown the deputies out of the window. Murat and Bonaparte have saved France."

* * *

At St Cloud the General was still busy. Although he had not eaten since the morning, he did not think of stopping now to dine.⁴⁴ In his opinion it was none too soon to get down to business. "The romance of the Revolution is finished," he told Sieyès and Roger-Ducos. "It is time to begin its history."

Talleyrand had less interest in history and more in his dinner. Shortly after the deputies had been ejected from the Orangery, he left St Cloud to dine at Sèvres with a friend, Madame Simons, an actress who was said to be one of Barras' mistresses. Quite a little group of like-minded people were there. Towards the close of the excellent meal, someone looked across at Talleyrand and said: "I understand our General wasn't quite up to snuff today, eh?"

If General Bonaparte had been less impressive than usual, however, Lucien had excelled himself. And he was still serving his brother's cause. When he heard that one of the deputies who had been driven from the Orangery had fled to the Council of Ancients to report what had occurred, Lucien at once went to the senior chamber and as President of the Five Hundred obtained permission to speak.

"You are imposed upon, citizens," he stated flatly. "The armed force which is said to have outraged the national representation consisted merely of a few grenadiers who, following their officers caused a slight movement in the Council."

Perhaps Lucien noticed some incredulity on the faces before him, for he continued in a somewhat different vein.

"Do you call assassins armed with poniards representatives? They attacked me, aided by accomplices who occupied the tribune.

The cannibals even wanted me to pronounce the outlawry of my brother! A handful of factious agitators tyrannised over the Council of Five Hundred, but the majority adhere to the Ancients and applauds its wisdom."[45]

Nevertheless in spite of Lucien's efforts, there were bitter recriminations in the Council of Ancients. The debate stopped only when Lemercier announced that he was adjourning the Assembly until nine o'clock, at which time it would hear the report of an extraordinary commission set up to investigate the occurrences of the day.

In Bonaparte's eyes, the clearing of the Orangery by the grenadiers had been a deplorable necessity. The only good thing about it was that the Guard of the Directory had done the work rather than the regular army. He hoped, however, that even now it might not be too late to disguise the *coup d'état* behind legal forms. Messengers were sent out into the darkness to round up all the Bonapartist deputies they could find and bring them back to St Cloud. Luckily, a number of representatives were discovered dining in a nearby café and a few more were found in the vicinity. All were hurried back to St Cloud, but when they were counted it was found that they totalled no more than thirty. Lucien promptly dubbed this rump of the Assembly the Majority of the Council and took his place again on the rostrum as President.

When the sessions met again, the public galleries in both Council Chambers were filled with army officers, Bonaparte's friends, and the élite of Parisian society. The spectators chattered and laughed among themselves as they ate the picnic lunches which the more thoughtful had taken care to provide. Perhaps the play was proving over long, but there had, after all, been numerous intermissions, and no one could say that it had not been interesting.

It was, in fact, almost over. In the Five Hundred, now reduced to thirty, the deputy Berenger rose to propose a vote of thanks to Generals Bonaparte, Lefèbvre and Murat and to the regiments which had so recently ejected his colleagues from the Hall.[46] At the same time, in the Council of Ancients, a motion was carried that the three provisional Consuls swear the oath of fidelity to the Republic. They did so in alphabetical order, Bonaparte swearing first, followed by Roger-Ducos and Sieyès.

In the Orangery Lucien made yet another speech, eloquently describing the dangers from which France had been saved.

" French liberty, born in the tennis-court at Versailles, has reached us, a prey to all the convulsive maladies of childhood, and this day has assumed maturity. All her agitations are henceforth at an end. Representatives of the people, listen to the sublime cry of posterity. If liberty was born on the tennis-court of Versailles, it was consolidated in the Orangery of St Cloud."[47]

Many of those who heard Lucien thought that he spoke very well.

And so the day ended with complete victory for the General. The Councils decreed that the Directory was at an end, that Bonaparte, Sieyès and Roger-Ducos were appointed Provisional Consuls, and that the Ancients and the Five Hundred adjourn until a new constitution could be drawn up.

Long after midnight the weary representatives at last took off their scarlet robes, picked up their hats and coats, and left St. Cloud. They were not to be needed again. To mark the occasion, however, Lucien later commissioned a portrait of himself, showing him standing in full costume in the Council of Five Hundred holding in his hand a scroll inscribed " 18th Brumaire."

While this was going on in the Assembly Halls, Bonaparte called his secretary and dictated a proclamation to the inhabitants of Paris. The wording of the proclamation shows that Bonaparte was quite himself again.

19 BRUMAIRE, YEAR VIII (10 NOV, 1799) PARIS 11 pm

On my return to Paris I found all authority in chaos and agreement only on the one truth that the Constitution was half destroyed and incapable of preserving liberty.

Men of every party came to me, confided their plans, disclosed their secrets and asked for my support: I refused to be a man of party.

The Council of the Ancients called upon me and I responded to its appeal. A plan for general reform has been drawn up by men upon whom the nation is accustomed to look as the defenders of liberty, equality and property. That plan needed calm examination, free from all fear and partisan influence. Therefore, the Council of the Ancients resolved to transfer the legislative body to Saint-Cloud and charged me to deploy the force necessary to ensure its independence. I believed it my duty to my fellow-citizens, to the soldiers laying down their lives in our armies, to the national glory gained at the price of their blood to accept this command.

The Councils reassembled at Saint-Cloud. The troops of the Republic guaranteed their security from without. But assassins created terror within. Several Deputies of the Council of Five Hundred, bearing daggers and fire-arms, uttered threats of death all around them. Discussion of the plans was halted, the majority became disorganized, the most intrepid orators hesitated and the hopelessness of any wise proposal was evident.

I carried my indignation and sorrow to the Council of the Ancients. I urged it to ensure the execution of its liberal designs. I recalled to it the ills of the nation which had led it to conceive them. The Council joined with me in renewed assurance of its steadfast resolve.

I then appeared before the Council of Five Hundred, alone, unarmed, bareheaded, just as the Ancients had received and applauded me. I came to recall the majority to its purpose and assure it of its power.

The daggers which threatened the deputies were immediately raised against their liberator: a score of assassins threw themselves upon me, seeking my breast. The grenadiers of the legislative guard, whom I had left at the door of the chamber, ran up, came between us and bore me out. One of the grenadiers had his coat pierced by a dagger.

At that moment cries of 'outlaw' were heard against the defender of the law, the savage cry of the assassins against the force destined to crush them. They pressed round the president, threatening, arms in their hands, ordering him to declare my outlawry. Told of this, I ordered him to be saved from their fury and six grenadiers rescued him. Immediately afterwards the legislative guard entered at the charge and cleared the chamber.

Intimidated, the seditious dispersed and disappeared. The majority, safe from their threats, returned freely and peacefully to the chamber, heard the proposals made to them for the public good, debated and prepared the salutary resolution which must become the new, provisional law of the Republic.

Frenchmen, you will no doubt recognise in my conduct the zeal of a soldier of liberty and of a devoted citizen of the Republic. Liberal, beneficent and traditional ideas have returned to their rightful place through the dispersal of the odious and despicable factions which sought to overawe the Councils.

BONAPARTE[48]

Fouché had this proclamation printed at once, and before morning it was posted up about Paris.

Now that General Bonaparte's *coup* had succeeded, the Minister of Police immediately began to consolidate his own position. He sat down in his office in Paris and prepared a report for Bonaparte on the state of affairs in the capital. He took care to draw to the General's attention the secret and malicious designs which he claimed Sieyès entertained against his colleague. Since one of Sieyès' first acts as a Provisional Consul was an attempt to have him removed from office, Fouché had good reason to be pleased with his foresight. He later said that the confidential report . . . " convinced [Bonaparte] that the police was as clear as it was quick sighted."[49] The General may well have looked at it in another way, but at all events he retained Fouché in charge of the police.

It was three o'clock in the morning of the 20th Brumaire before the General left St Cloud. During the drive back to Paris with his secretary, he sat exhausted and silent with his head sunk on his breast. Near the capital the General's carriage passed the marching columns of infantry going back to their barracks. The men were in good spirits and sang as they marched—

> *Ça ira, ça ira*
> *Les aristocrates à la lanterne*
> *Ça ira*
> *On les pendra.*

Josephine was in bed when the General arrived home. After he and Bourrienne had visited her bed-chamber to assure her that the *coup* had ended well, the General turned to his secretary and asked: " Bourrienne, did I say a great many ridiculous things?"

" Not so very bad, General."

" I prefer to speak to soldiers rather than to lawyers. Those fellows disconcerted me. I have not been used to public assemblies, but that will come in time." The General yawned. " Goodnight, Bourrienne," he said. " By the way, we shall sleep in the Luxembourg tomorrow."[50]

*　　*　　*

After no more than a few hours' sleep, Bonaparte was up and about again, applying himself to his new task with an amazing energy. The events of the 18th and 19th Brumaire had left the Parisians interested but not impassioned. One of them, who had been a spectator in the gallery of the Orangery, later wrote: " On my return, I found Paris as quiet as if nothing had happened, or as if St Cloud were four hundred kilometres away."[51]

On the morning of 20th Brumaire the General sent his brother Louis to release Gohier from protective arrest in the Luxembourg. This was not an entirely disinterested gesture. As President of the Directory Gohier had the best suite in the building, and Bonaparte wanted it for himself.

Gohier therefore left his luxuriously appointed apartment and took up lodgings elsewhere in Paris. Strangely enough, the former President evinced no gratitude for the General's clemency. For a long time Gohier went around telling everyone who would listen how easily the *coup* might have been prevented.

" We should have smitten him," he would say. " We should have smitten him without pity. If my advice had been taken, everything would have been easily settled."[52]

The General was quite willing to let Gohier talk as he liked, since he could now do no harm.

Bonaparte called the first meeting of the Provisional Consulate on the evening of 20th Brumaire. Any procedural difficulty as to who was to take the chair was resolved by Roger-Ducos before the meeting opened. He stood up when the General entered the room and offered him the presidential seat, saying that it was his by natural right. Sieyès could do nothing but acquiesce, although he must have felt suddenly isolated. Roger-Ducos, the born disciple, had obviously transferred his allegiance to another master.

It soon became apparent that Bonaparte had very definite ideas on how to reorganize France. Berthier replaced Dubois de Crancé as Minister of War; Talleyrand became Minister of Foreign Affairs; Fouché retained control of the police; Gaudin was made Minister of Finance; and Laplace, the famous astronomer and mathematician, received the Ministry of the Interior. Laplace soon proved himself incompetent as an administrator, however, and the Ministry of the Interior then went to Lucien Bonaparte as a reward for his services. Marmont was made a Counsellor of State, and Murat and Lannes were both promoted in the Consular Guard.

The first Consular meeting left Sieyès and Roger-Ducos more than a little breathless. They were not accustomed to conducting business with quite so much speed and despatch. After the meeting Sieyès happened to meet Talleyrand, Roederer and Chazal. Sieyès looked at them wryly. " Gentlemen," he said, " you have found a master."[53]

Although Bonaparte's policy had been to abolish all oppressive acts, on 26th Brumaire, at Sieyès' instigation, a list of fifty-nine proscribed Jacobins was promulgated. Thirty-seven of them were condemned to exile in French Guiana and twenty-two to the Island of Oleron. Jourdan was one of those sentenced to banishment.

Each of the three Jacobin generals who had refused to take part in the *coup d'état* had reacted in his own way to Bonaparte's success. Jourdan had left St Cloud after the deputies had been driven from the Orangery and hidden in the house of a friend until he thought it safe to emerge. Bernadotte, for all the world like some character in a Shakespearean comedy, is said to have sought refuge in the forest of Senart near Villeneuve St Georges, taking poor little Désirée with him disguised as a boy. Augereau remained where he was, blandly pretended that he had been on Bonaparte's side all along, and was one of the first to congratulate him.

Because Bonaparte was determined to stamp out party feeling in France and unite the country as a single weapon in his own hand, he insisted on cancelling Sieyès' order for the deportation of the Jacobin deputies.[54] The sentences were all mitigated before they were put into effect. Many of the proscribed deputies were released outright, and the remainder were merely placed under police surveillance in their own districts. Just over a year later, however, when Bonaparte narrowly escaped death from an infernal machine which was exploded near his carriage on Christmas Eve, many of those who had opposed 18th Brumaire were among the one hundred and thirty republicans to be interned or exiled to Guiana.

Shortly after the *coup d'état*, Bonaparte discovered a chest filled with gold which had been used as a secret fund for the Directory. He turned it over to Sieyès with the comment that, if he knew nothing about it officially, he would not have to confiscate it for the state; Sieyès and Roger-Ducos could then divide it between them. The money promptly disappeared, but it is certain that Roger-Ducos saw very little of it.[55] This was quite agreeable to Bonaparte, for the ex-abbé was henceforth in his power.

By now Sieyès' new constitution was almost ready. Under it the supreme power would be placed in the hands of two Consuls, one for peace and one for war, and there was no doubt that Sieyès intended these posts to be filled by himself and General Bonaparte. " Nothing can be done with fools and drivellers," Sieyès had said before the *coup*. " We only need two things, a headpiece and a sword."[56] Sieyès was foolish enough still to hope that the General might be content to be the sword, while he himself acted as the headpiece for France. For a short time there appeared to be grounds for this hope. On 19th Brumaire two Commissions appointed from the Council of Ancients and the Five Hundred had been charged with revising the Constitution of the Year III, and at first both Commissions intended to recommend the adoption of Sieyès' constitution.

This did not suit Bonaparte at all. Having come thus far, he had no intention of sharing power with anyone. Accordingly, he had some of his supporters draw up a rival constitution more in keeping with his own ideas, and had this document secretly countersigned by members of both Commissions before he showed it to Sieyès and Roger-Ducos. By its terms there would be one First Consul—obviously Bonaparte—who would promulgate laws, nominate all senior officials, control finances, decide on peace or war, and conduct all negotiations with foreign states. Two other Consuls would be no more than advisers to the First Consul. Beneath the Consulate there would be a Legislature consisting of a Senate, a Council of State, a Tribunate and a Legislative Body, but these assemblies would have no real powers. What was proposed was, in fact, an out-and-out dictatorship.

On the night of 12th December this constitution of Bonaparte's was countersigned by the three Provisional Consuls and promulgated. It came into effect on Christmas Day, 1799.

Sieyès left Paris to take up residence on a country estate he had purchased near Versailles.[57] Roger-Ducos, who had never much liked the business of governing in any case, was glad enough to tender his resignation as well. Cambacérès became Second Consul, and Lebrun, a nonentity chosen because he could be counted on to agree with Bonaparte, was made Third Consul.

The French Revolution was over.

Epilogue

LITTLE NEED be said of the technique of the *coup*. All the important details had been determined before Bonaparte entered the conspiracy, and almost certainly this accounts for the technical weaknesses of the plan. If Bonaparte had had the ordering of affairs from the beginning it is unlikely that the *coup* would have been spread over two days or that the secret would have been shared among so many.

On the other hand, most of Bonaparte's difficulties on the 19th Brumaire were of his own making and sprang from the contradiction inherent in his aims. He desired the results of an illegal act; but he wanted to have them without resorting to illegality. He had long intended to make himself the head of the French government—and to his mind this was synonymous with being the absolute master of France. For this, it was essential that France be unified; Bonaparte had no use for a splintered sword. A simple military seizure of power, he thought, might indefinitely delay the unification of the nation, and in the hope of avoiding this he was willing to endure the discussions and delays of the 18th and 19th Brumaire. As it turned out, of course, he miscalculated, for he was able to rally virtually all Frenchmen behind him even after he had driven their elected representatives from the Orangery at bayonet point.

Some historians have been mystified by Bonaparte's apparent incompetence on 19th Brumaire and have advanced various theories to account for it. Unfortunately, these explanations are often more mysterious than the mystery itself. The reasons for the scene in the Council of Five Hundred when Bonaparte was dragged fainting from the Hall are surely obvious enough. After the intense activity of the 18th Brumaire and the days immediately preceding it, Bonaparte must have been close to nervous exhaustion. Add to this that he was a small man who was being very roughly manhandled by a number of deputies, including the gigantic Destrem, and the fainting spell can easily be accounted for by purely physical causes. No momentary cowardice need be imputed to a man who so frequently proved himself of an exemplary courage.

More interesting, perhaps, is the question of why the General made such a poor showing in his speech before the Council of Ancients. Again, the simplest explanation is probably the best, and there is no reason to believe that Bonaparte's breakdown was due to anything except ordinary stage-fright. He had never before addressed a hostile audience ; the hecklers threw him off his stride ; and the palpable weakness of his case was no doubt an additional cause for nervousness.

Other theories have been advanced—that for once in his life he played the coward, that he was suddenly stricken by a sense of guilt, or that he was momentarily overwhelmed by the magnitude of the stakes involved. None of these explanations is in the least plausible. Bonaparte was as much a stranger to guilt as to cowardice, and a great deal of his future success was due to his always being prepared to gamble with all he had won. Moreover, on 18th and 19th Brumaire, he always had, as a last resource, an absolute superiority of force. In spite of what some of his supporters subsequently said, the ultimate issue of the *coup d'état* was never in doubt, for the regular army would have obeyed him. The only issue that really had to be decided was whether or not the Directory could be overthrown without violence.

The importance of the part played by Lucien does not require emphasis. He always claimed that he had saved the day for his brother, although Napoleon was later to belittle his contribution. Perhaps Napoleon may be forgiven for this, both because he had been more aware than Lucien of the soldiers in the courtyard at St Cloud and because, as has been truly pointed out,[1] Lucien's work on 19th Brumaire was the only occasion when any member of the Bonaparte family ever helped in any way to forward Napoleon's career. That family was better, as a rule, at quarrelling over the spoils—as though, in Napoleon's own neat phrase, " they were being cheated out of the patrimony of our late father, the King."[2]

In any case, the country was certainly right in its instinctive belief that the *coup d'état* was Napoleon's. Lucien might tell his friends how well his own conduct contrasted with his brother's ; Talleyrand's intimates might indulge in polished eighteenth century sneers about the General not being up to snuff; but France accepted the 18th Brumaire with positive enthusiasm. The French people considered the most extravagant praise of the General not unseemly, for they were frankly overjoyed to see the Revolution at an end. There had been too much oppression and bloodshed, too much windy talk, too much amateur philosophizing, too much venality and corruption, too much inefficiency, and, above all, too much insecurity. It was time for a right turn.

In his military campaigns General Bonaparte was wont to tell his subordinate commanders: " Ask me anything but time! " After 18th Brumaire he applied the same principle to civil affairs. When the new Minister of Finance, Gaudin, was summoned to the Council Chamber the day after the *coup d'état*, Bonaparte asked him: " Have you been dealing with financial matters a long time?"

" For twenty years, General," Gaudin replied.

" We need your co-operation very badly," Bonaparte said. " I shall count on you. Take the oath quickly, as we are in a hurry."

Yet, although for the time being nothing but good appeared to have resulted from 18th Brumaire, in the end other things had to be taken into account as well. The *coup* had been illegal. It had been a product of violence and duplicity—and it put in

power, as was only to be expected, a man who in the last analysis
was committed to violence and duplicity. Men were later to claim
that Bonaparte was slowly transformed from a good into a bad
despot, that the intransigence of the kings, the relentless hatred
of England, and a host of impersonal historical forces drove him
steadily down a darkening road to defeat and disaster. There is
some truth in this view, but it ignores the character of the man of
Brumaire. And for him, even more than for most of us, his
character was his destiny.

All the subsequent history of the Napoleonic epoch—the
nations invaded, the lands laid waste, the thrones overturned, the
men who were to die, the women who were to weep—all flowed,
as it were inevitably, from 18th Brumaire. The fate of Europe
narrowed, and concentrated, and focused, until it was little more
than the personality of one man. The French henceforth lived
under a hard, bright sun where everything appeared clear-cut,
sharply outlined, and often brilliant. But it was a desert sun,
and it killed all initiative and all creativeness. Napoleon himself
was not unaware of this. He remarked once: " People say we have
no literature. That is the fault of the Minister of the Interior."
After the 18th Brumaire there was, in truth, room in France for
only one creative intelligence. Bonaparte was to rule in the same
way as he had come to power; he was always to put too much
faith in his sword, to seek the solution for all problems too much
in violence or in the sudden astounding stroke of treachery. He
was the eternal opportunist, ever ready to shift his opinions or his
policies if such a shift would consolidate or increase his power.
From the moment when Murat's soldiers cleared the Orangery,
France began to be recreated in the Napoleonic image as a military society under an absolute sovereign.

There followed after 18th Brumaire a decade and a half of
brilliant victories, interspersed here and there with the occasional
defeat—Marengo, Austerlitz, Jena, Friedland, Wagram—but also
Aspern-Essling, Salamanca, the retreat from Moscow, Leipzig,
and at the end, Waterloo. At the end France lost all her

conquests, including those that had been won by the Revolution. She was left surrounded by a Europe awakened to nationalism and deeply hostile to her as a warlike aggressor. She was left, by way of compensation, the memory of the Napoleonic epic, the roll-call of glorious names, the pride of arms, and—much more dubiously—the Napoleonic Legend.

Perhaps it was best summed up by Lucien, who quarrelled with his brother not long after the 18th Brumaire and was reconciled with him only at the end, during the Hundred Days. Looking back on all the incredible events that had followed the *coup d'état*, his comment was: "What memories! What regrets!"

Of the five marshals who had accompanied Bonaparte back from Egypt, four paid with their lives for having followed their General's star. Lannes was struck on the knee by a cannon-ball at Aspern-Essling in May 1809. His leg was amputated, but his condition gradually worsened as he lay for nine days in the improvised hospital in Vienna. In his delirium, Lannes called for his guns, ordered his *cuirassiers* to charge, and formed up his columns of grenadiers to attack imaginary battle-lines. Then suddenly he awoke to a brief consciousness. He rested his head on the shoulder of his young aide-de-camp, Captain de Marbot, the same boy whom he had befriended at Lyons ten years before while he was on his way to Paris with General Bonaparte. After asking to be remembered to his wife and children, Jean Lannes sighed, turned his face to the wall, and died.

Bessières was the next to fall, in May 1813, at Lützen. He had a premonition of death, and on the morning of the battle he gloomily burned all his wife's love letters before riding out to be killed by a Prussian field-gun. Berthier, who never married his beloved Madame Visconti, abandoned Napoleon after his exile to Elba. During the Hundred Days, Berthier, jumped to his death from a high window in Bamberg when he heard Russian gun-carriages rattling over the cobblestones in the street below and realized that in the last campaign he would not be by Napoleon's side.

Murat, flamboyant to the last, made a desperate attempt to regain his lost throne of Naples in the autumn of 1815. A storm scattered his tiny flotilla and he was driven ashore at Pizzo on the coast of Calabria with only twenty-six followers. The same afternoon that he landed he was arrested, hurriedly court-martialled, and condemned to die. There, standing against a mud wall on the outskirts of a filthy little village, the greatest cavalry commander of all time faced the firing squad with characteristic swagger and vanity. Long ago in Egypt he had written home to tell the girls that his wound at the Battle of Aboukir had not impaired his looks, and now as he stood against the wall his last words to his executioners were: "Soldiers, do your duty. Fire at my heart, but spare the face." His wife, who at the time of 18th Brumaire had been Bonaparte's schoolgirl sister, Caroline, did not mourn him long.

Marmont, the unluckiest of them all, betrayed Napoleon in 1814. He got little good from it, for the French despised him, and after the Bourbons were expelled in 1830, he lingered on, an unhappy exile wandering from country to country, until he died in Venice in 1852.

Of those most intimately associated with Bonaparte at the time of 18th Brumaire, only Talleyrand gained any lasting profit from the *coup*. Once when Napoleon asked him how he had made so much money so quickly, Talleyrand, not a whit disconcerted, smilingly replied: "Ah Sire, I bought stock on 17th Brumaire and sold it on 19th."[3]

Yet it is sometimes argued that the *coup* was necessary, that the government of the Directory was too impossible to be allowed to live. Napoleon, of course, argued this himself. On St Helena he said: "People are still engaged in abstract deliberation as to whether our action of 18th Brumaire was a legal or a criminal one. At the best, however, these are but theories suitable for books or public orators, and which disappear before the face of sheer necessity. It is like condemning a sailor for chopping off a mast to escape shipwreck. The perpetrators of this great *coup d'état* could reply to their accusers as did the Roman of old: 'Our act is justified in that we saved the Republic ; let us therefore render thanks to the gods.' "⁴

There is strength in this argument, although it is by no means a quibble to point out that whatever 18th Brumaire did or did not achieve, it certainly did *not* save the Republic. The answer, however, surely is that so long as some form of representative government existed, there had always been the possibility of reform and of the retention of individual liberty.

After 18th Brumaire this was no longer possible. The genie was out of the bottle, and it took all Europe fifteen years and more to put him back again. And so, in spite of his incredible energy, his courage and power of decision, his industry, his fantastic memory, and in spite of the almost unparalleled breadth and quickness of his understanding—in spite of all these qualities (nay rather, almost because of them) it was a real tragedy for France and the world that 18th Brumaire was successful.

It would perhaps have been better if there really had been poniards drawn that November afternoon in the Orangery.

References

In addition to the primary sources cited in the References, the following are among the books consulted.

Geyl, Pieter, *Napoleon : For and Against*, (trans. Olive Renier) (London, 1949).

Kircheisen, F. M., *Napoleon* (trans. Henry St Lawrence) (London, 1931).

Lanfrey, P., *The History of Napoleon the First*, (4 vols., London, 1886).

Macdonnel, A. G., *Napoleon and His Marshals* (London, 1934).

Masson, Frédéric, *Mme Bonaparte (1796–1804)*, (Paris, 1920).
       —*Napoléon et sa famille*, (vol. I., Paris, 1897).

Morton, J. B., *Brumaire : the Rise of Napoleon*, (London, 1948).

Ollivier, Albert, *Le Dix-huit brumaire*, (Paris, 1959).

Seignobos, Charles, *Histoire sincère de la Nation française*, (Paris, 1930).

Sterling, Monica, *Pride of Lions*, (London, 1961).

Thompson, J. M., *Napoleon Bonaparte : His Rise and Fall*, (Oxford, 1952).

Vandal, Count Albert, *L'avènement de Bonaparte*, (2 vols., Paris, 1903).

PART ONE—Pages 13 to 51

1. *Mémoires du duc de Rovigo : pour servir à l'histoire de L'Empereur Napoléon,* (ed. Désirée Lacroix) (5 vols., Paris, 1900), I, 140n.
2. *Ibid ;* Bourrienne, Louis Antoine Fauvelet de, *Mémoires de Napoléon Bonaparte,* (3 vols., Paris, n.d.), I, 247.
3. Quoted in: Haydon, Benjamin Robert, *The Diary of Benjamin Robert Haydon,* (ed. Tom Taylor) (5 vols., Cambridge, Mass., 1960), I, 199–200.
4. Miot de Mélito, André François, *Mémoires du Comte de Melito,* (2 vols., Paris, 1858), II, 32.
5. *Correspondance de Napoléon I,* (32 vols., Paris, 1858–70), V, No. 4225.
6. Bourrienne, I, 240.
7. Marmont, Auguste Frédéric Louis Viesse de, *Mémoires du Maréchal duc de Raguse de 1792 à 1832,* (9 vols., Paris, 1857), II, 32–5.
8. *Correspondance de Napoléon I, V,* No. 4366.
9. duc de Rovigo, I, 141.
10. *Correspondance de Napoléon I, V,* No. 4374.
11. *Ibid.,* No. 4380.
12. Beauharnais, Eugene, *Mémoires et Correspondance Politique et Militaire de Prince Eugene,* (ed. A. du Casse) (Paris, 1858), I, 72.
13. *Ibid.*
14. *Correspondance de Napoléon I,* Bulletin No. 29, the Emperor Napoleon to the Grand Army, Molodetchno, 3 December, 1812.
15. Las Cases, E. A. D. M. J., Marquis de, *Le Mémorial de Sainte-Hélène : journal ou se trouve consigné, jour par jour ce qu'a dit et fait Napoléon durant dix-huit mois,* (9 vols., Paris, 1840), I, 166

16. Marmont, II, 45; duc de Rovigo, I, 141.
17. *Ibid.*
18. Bourrienne, I, 247-8.
19. Eugene, I, 73.
20. Marmont, II, 43-4.
21. Madame Junot, *The Autobiography and Recollections of Laura, Duchess of Abrantes (widow of General Junot) : with Reminiscences of her Life in Corsica, Paris, and in Spain and Portugal,* (4 vols., New York, 1894), I, 335.
22. *Ibid.*
23. *Le Mémorial de Sainte-Hélène,* III, 24.
24. Marmont, I, 41.
25. Eugene, I, 73.
26. Bourrienne, I, 253.
27. Madame Junot, I, 331-4.
28. *Letters de Napoléon à Joséphine pendant la premiere campagne d'Italie, le Consulat et l'Empire et lettres de Joséphine à Napoléon et sa fille* (Mémoires Historiques et Militaires sur la Révolution, le Consulat et l'Empire), (Paris, n.d.), Napoleon to Josephine, Verona, le 3 frimaire An V (13 Nov 1796), 19.
29. *Mémoires et Correspondance Politique et Militaire du Roi Joseph,* (ed. A. du Casse) (Paris, 1855), I, 189.
30. Eugene, I, 45 ; Bourrienne, I, 183-4.
31. Bourrienne, I, 176.
32. Bertrand, Henrie-Gratien, *Napoleon at St. Helena : the Journals of General Bertrand from January to May of 1821, deciphered and annotated by Paul Fleuriot de Langle,* (trans. Frances Hume) (New York, 1952), 92, 280.
33. *Mémoires de Fouché,* (2 vols., Paris, 1825), I, 37.
34. *Ibid.*
35. Bourrienne, I, 249-50.
36. Marmont, II, 45-6.
37. *Ibid.*
38. Madame Junot, I, 21.
39. Masson, F., *Napoléon Inconnu,* Note of 3 May, 1786, I, 145.
40. Méneval, Claude-Francois, Baron de, *Memoirs to Serve for the History of Napoleon I from 1802 to 1815,* (3 vols., London, 1895), I, 8-10.

41. Bourrienne, I, 250–1.
42. Marmont, II, 53; Bertrand, 102.
43. Bourrienne, I, 251.
44. Fouché, I, 79.
45. Laravellière-Lépeaux, *Mémoires*, II, ch.x/iv.
46. Fouché, I, 80.
47. Bourrienne, I, 253.
48. *Ibid.*
49. de Méneval, I, 10 ; duc de Rovigo, I, 170n.
50. Marmont, II, 46–7.
51. Bourrienne, I, 254.
52. duc de Rovigo, I, 172n.
53. Marmont, II, 55–6.
54. *Correspondance de Napoléon I*, V, No. 4382.
55. Marbot, Lieutenant-General Baron de, *The Memoirs of Baron de Marbot*, (trans. A. J. Butler) (London, 1913), 24–9.
56. Constant, *Mémoires de Constant, premier valet de chambre de Napoléon Ier*, (3 vols., Paris, n.d.), I, 291.

PART TWO—Pages 52 to 106

1. Marmont, II, 91.
2. *Memoirs of Lucien Bonaparte, Prince of Casino,* (London, 1835), 78.
3. *Le Mémorial de Sainte-Hélène,* III, 24.
4. Madame Junot, I, 254.
5. Constant, I, 330–1.
6. Miot de Mélito, I, 101–2 ; de Méneval, I, 27.
7. Fouché, I, 90.
8. *Ibid.,* 75.
9. *Ibid.,* 86.
10. Marmont, II, 51.
11. Lucien Bonaparte, 76.
12. Barras, *Memoirs of Barras, Member of the Directorate* (ed. George Daruy) (trans. Charles E. Roche) (4 vols., London, 1895), IV, 36.
13. Madame Junot, I, 265.
14. *Ibid.,* II, 124–5.
15. Bourrienne, I, 258.
16. *Ibid.,* 262.
17. Madame Junot, I, 266.
18. Bourrienne, I, 262.
19. Gohier, L., *Mémoires de Louis-Jérome Gohier, Président du Directoire au 18 brumaire,* (2 vols., Paris, 1824), I, 201.
20. Constant, I, 257–8.
21. Gohier, I, 201.
22. Barras, *Mémoires,* IV, 45.
23. Bourrienne, I, 277.
24. Gohier, I, 202.
25. Barras, IV, 39–43.
26. Madame Junot, I, 267–8.

27. Madame de Rémusat, *Memoirs : 1802–1808,* (ed. Paul de Rémusat) (trans. Mrs. Cashel Hoey and John Lillie) (3 vols., New York, 1880), I, 28–9.
28. Lucien Bonaparte, 70.
29. Marmont, I, 89.
30. Madame de Rémusat, I, 100.
31. Gohier, I, 202.
32. *Ibid.,* 204.
33. Bourrienne, I, 277 ; Thiébault, Général, *Mémoires du Géneral bon Thiébault : publées sous les auspicis de sa fille, Mlle Claire Thiébault d'apres le manuscrit original,* (5 vols., Paris, 1895). III, 59.
34. Gohier, *Mémoires,* I, 206–10.
35. Fouché, I, 94.
36. *Ibid.,* 97–8.
37. Marmont, I, 92.
38. Madame de Rémusat, I, 9.
39. Barras, IV, 44.
40. Bourrienne, I, 267.
41. Madame Junot, I, 81–2.
42. Bourrienne, I, 252.
43. *Ibid.,* 277.
44. *Ibid.,* 270.
45. Fouché, 99–100.
46. *Ibid.*
47. *Mémoires du Roi Joseph,* I, 77.
48. Bourrienne, I, 271–2.
49. Roederer, *Oeuvres du Comte P. L. Roederer,* (8 vols., Paris, 1854), *Notice de ma Vie, pour mes enfants,* III, 296.
50. Lucien Bonaparte, 68 ; Madame Junot, II, 228.
51. Fouché, I, 102.
52. *Ibid.,* 102–3.
53. Bourrienne, I, 279.
54. *Mémoires du Prince de Talleyrand,* (ed. le duc de Broglie) (Paris, 1891), 272n.
55. *Mémoires d'un pair de France,* (Paris, 1830), III, 14.
56. Lucien Bonaparte, 78–9.

57. Fouché, I, 107.
58. Bourrienne, I, 280–1.
59. *Mémoires du Roi Joseph,* I, 78.
60. Fouché, I, 101.
61. Cornet, *Notice sur le 18 brumaire.*

PART THREE—Pages 107 to 163

1. Madame de Rémusat, III, 570n.
2. Bourrienne, I, 282. (Note, however, that this account is contradicted by Joseph, *Erreurs*, I, 252 and *Memoires*, I, 78.)
3. Barras, IV, 92–3 ; Bourrienne, I, 281–7.
4. Fouché, I, 106–9.
5. *Ibid.*, 110–11.
6. *Ibid.*, 108–9.
7. *Ibid.*, 110.
8. Eugene, I, 77.
9. Madame Junot, I, 416.
10. Marmont, I, 292–3.
11. Thiébault, A. C., *Le Consulat et L'Empire : ou Histoire de la France et de Napoléon Bonaparte de 1799 à 1815*, (4 vols., Paris, 1834), I, 26–7.
12. Fouché, I, 110.
13. Marmont, II, 95–6.
14. *Ibid.*, 113.
15. *Ibid.*, 113–14.
16. *Ibid.*, 115.
17. Madame Junot, I, 274.
18. Gohier, I, 228.
19. Bourrienne, I, 285.
20. Madame Junot, I, 270–6.
21. Fouché, I, 116.
22. *Ibid.*, 117.
23. Bourrienne, I, 285.
24. Barras, IV, 110.
25. Bourrienne, I, 287.
26. Madame de Rémusat, I, 29.
27. Fouché, I, 118.

28. Bourrienne, I, 287.
29. Fouché, I, 119.
30. Thiébault, III, 68–9.
31. *Mémoires du Roi Joseph,* I, 79.
32. Bourrienne, I, 287.
33. Thiébault, I, 44.
34. Bourrienne, I, 290.
35. Thibaudeau, I, 40–1
36. Bourrienne, I, 29–30.
37. Thiébault, III, 60.
38. Bourrienne, I, 292.
39. Fouché, I, 121.
40. Bourrienne, I, 293.
41. Lucien Bonaparte, 79.
42. Bourrienne, I, 295–6 ; Lucien Bonaparte, 80.
43. Madame Junot, I, 276–7.
44. Bourrienne, I, 297.
45. Lucien Bonaparte, 82–3.
46. *Ibid.,* 84.
47. *Ibid.,* 87.
48. *Correspondance de Napoléon Ier,* VI, 6–8.
49. Fouché, I, 128.
50. Bourrienne, I, 302.
51. Thibaudeau, *Mémoires: le Directoire,* (Paris, 1824), I, 68.
52. Madame Junot, I, 279.
53. Fouché, I, 126.
54. *Ibid.,* 130–1.
55. *Ibid.,* 126.
56. *Ibid.,* 71.
57. Bourrienne, I, 311n.

EPILOGUE—Pages 165 to 171

1. Geyl, Pieter, *Napoleon : For and Against,* (London, 1949), 187.
2. Madame de Rémusat, I, 171 ; *Memoirs of General de Caulaincourt, Duke of Vicenzo,* (3 vols., London, 1935), II, 228.
3. Madame de Rémusat, I, 85.
4. *Le Mémorial de Sainte-Hélène,* III, 5–6.

Appendix

PROCLAMATION
Paris, 19 brumaire an viii (10 novembre 1799), 11 heures du soir.

A mon retour à Paris, j'ai trouvé la division dans toutes les autorités, et l'accord établi sur cette vérité, que la Constitution était à moitié détruite et ne pouvait sauver la liberté.

Tous les partis sont venus à moi, m'ont confié leurs desseins, dévoilé leurs secrets, et m'ont demandé mon appui : j'ai refusé d'être l'homme d'un parti.

Le Conseil des Anciens m'a appelé : j'ai répondu à son appel. Un plan de restauration générale avait été concerté par des hommes en qui la nation est accoutumée à voir des défenseurs de la liberté, de l'égalité, de la propriété: ce plan demandait un examen calme, libre, exempt de toute influence et de toute crainte. En conséquence, le Conseil des Anciens a résolu la translation du corps législatif à Saint-Cloud; il m'a chargé de la disposition de la force nécessaire à son indépendance. J'ai cru devoir à mes concitoyens, aux soldats périssant dans nos armées, à la gloire nationale acquise au prix de leur sang, d'accepter le commandement.

Les Conseils se rassemblent à Saint-Cloud; les troupes républicaines garantissent la sûreté au dehors; mais des assassins établissent la terreur au dedans. Plusieurs députés du Conseil des Cinq-Cents, armés de stylets et d'armes à feu, font circuler tout autour d'eux des menaces de mort.

Les plans qui devaient être développés sont resserrés, la majorité désorganisée, les orateurs les plus intrépides déconcertés, et l'inutilité de toute proposition sage évidente.

Je porte mon indignation et ma douleur au Conseil des Anciens. Je lui demande d'assurer l'exécution de ses généreux desseins; je lui représente les maux de la patrie qui les lui ont fait concevoir ; il s'unit à moi par de nouveaux témoignages de sa constante volonté.

Je me présente au Conseil des Cinq-Cents, seul, sans armes, la tête découverte, tel que les Anciens m'avaient reçu et applaudi ; je venais rappeler à la majorité ses volontés et l'assurer de son pouvoir.

Les stylets qui menaçaient les députés sont aussitôt levés sur leur libérateur; vingt assassins se précipitent sur moi et cherchent ma poitrine. Les grenadiers du corps législatif, que j'avais laissés à la porte de la salle, accourent, se mettent entre les assassins et moi. L'un de ces grenadiers[1] est frappé d'un coup de stylet dont ses habits sont percés. Ils m'enlèvent !

Au même moment, les cris de *hors la loi* se font entendre contre le défenseur de la loi. C'était le cri farouche des assassins contre la force destinée à les réprimer.

Ils se pressent autour du président, la menace à la bouche, les armes à la main; ils lui ordonnent de prononcer le *hors la loi ;* l'on m'avertit; je donne ordre de l'arracher à leur fureur, et six grenadiers du corps législatif s'en emparent. Aussitôt après, des grenadiers du corps législatif entrent au pas de charge dans la salle et la font évacuer.

Les factieux, intimidés, se dispersent et s'éloignent. La majorité, soustraite à leurs coups, rentre librement et paisiblement dans la salle de ses séances, entend les propositions qui devaient lue être faites pour le salut public, délibère et prépare la résolution salutaire qui doit devenir la loi nouvelle et provisoire de la République.

Français, vous reconnaîtrez sans doute à cette conduite le zèle d'un soldat de la liberté, d'un citoyen dévoué à la République.

Les idées conservatrices, tutélaires, libérales, sont rentrées dans leurs droits par la dispersion des factieux qui opprimaient les Conseils, et qui, pour être devenus les plus odieux des hommes, n'ont pas cessé d'en être les plus méprisables.

BONAPARTE.

[1] Thomé.
Extrait du *Moniteur.*

Index